Born Again to Win

Michael McComb, D. Min.

TRILOGY CHRISTIAN PUBLISHERS
TUSTIN, CA

Trilogy Christian Publishers
A Wholly Owned Subsidary of Trinity Broadcasting Network
2442 Michelle Drive
Tustin, CA 92780

Born Again to Win

Unless otherwise noted, all scripture quotations are from the NKJ Bible.

For information, address Trilogy Christian Publishing

Rights Department, 2442 Michelle Drive, Tustin, Ca 92780.

Trilogy Christian Publishing/ TBN and colophon are trademarks of Trinity Broadcasting Network.

For information about special discounts for bulk purchases, please contact Trilogy Christian Publishing.

Cover image taken by author:

Weminuche Wilderness in the San Juan National Forest; Mineral County, Colorado (2020). All rights reserved.

Manufactured in the United States of America

Trilogy Disclaimer: The views and content expressed in this book are those of the author and may not necessarily reflect the views and doctrine of Trilogy Christian Publishing or the Trinity Broadcasting Network.

10 9 8 7 6 5 4 3 2 1

Library of Congress Cataloging-in-Publication Data is available.

ISBN 978-1-63769-362-9

ISBN 978-1-63769-363-6 (ebook)

Contents

Dedication

To all who read this book,

May the truths shared in these pages see your faith strengthened, bring revelation of the benefits that are yours in Christ, and see you empowered by and enjoying the presence of the Holy Spirit.

You Were Born Again to Win!

Acknowledgements

"I want to express my appreciation to a few people who have helped me so much. My love and gratitude go to my dear wife Stephanie for her support and help editing, proofreading, and providing quality assurance with each devotion I have written.

Also, my heartfelt appreciation goes to our mentors and dear friends, prison evangelists "Rappin'" Ron Brigmon, and his beautiful wife, Miss Katie! They have mentored me/us in prison ministry and have provided the example and inspiration for writing these devotionals. Thank you for believing in me and encouraging me in this effort. I will forever owe you a debt of gratitude! Stephanie and I love and appreciate you so much.

As a graduate of Charis Bible College, I must acknowledge and express thankfulness to my favorite Bible teacher, Andrew Wommack. I have gleaned and assimilated his deep and meaningful teachings, which are evident in my preaching, teaching, and writing. I am profoundly grateful.

There have been many men of God who have spoken into my life and helped shape me spiritually. For that, I am thankful as well.

Last, but not least, I am so *very thankful* for the leading and inspiration of the Holy Spirit and His help to accomplish this work. Amen!

Foreword

Dr. Mike McComb's 100-day devotional, *Born Again to Win*, is a must for new believers and a tool for mature believers to grow and disciple others. One of the most important teachings for new believers is to know who God is and to know who they are as His child. The fundamentals of faith and grace are easily explained and resonate throughout this devotional. The overcomer mentality is prevalent throughout, as described by its title.

As we began to read Dr. McComb's devotionals, we were super impressed with the quality, substance, and excellence demonstrated in his literary gift. As a Chaplain, he has shared these truths with inmates for years. We are so delighted that he is offering them now to the whole body of Christ.

We highly recommend *Born Again to Win* to anyone wanting to grow spiritually in their walk with Christ.

Ron and Katie Brigmon
Ron Brigmon Ministries
https://www.ronbrigmon.com/

Introduction

I have had a long-held desire to write a book on the nuggets of truth from God's Word that I hold so dear. The book you hold in your hand is the fulfillment of that desire. I began to write devotions during the COVID-19 pandemic, which shut down ministry in the prisons. My aim was to use these devotionals to keep ministry flowing to the church that I pastored behind the prison walls. I began to feel compelled to continue as I believed God was inspiring me to accomplish this work.

Each devotion is designed to be a teaching from the Word. I believe the devotions contained in this work have the potential to really bless your life. The reason I strongly believe this is when I was a new Christian, I was struggling financially. I was so poor I could not spare the extra money to buy books from the bookstore at our church. A full-size book sold for $5.00 in those days, but I just did not feel I could spare that much to buy a book when I needed the money to buy milk for my children! However, I felt I could spend the fifty cents for the mini-books they offered authored by ministers I held in high esteem. I read those mini-books over and over until I understood them well. I now consider them to have been instrumental in establishing a solid faith foundation in my life!

I have experienced firsthand how the short but powerful teachings can influence and establish a person's understanding of spiritual truths. Discipleship has been my passion for many years. It is something which is often neglected in people's lives these days. Jesus said in John 8:31–32, *"...If you abide in My word, you are My disciples indeed. And you shall know the truth, and the truth shall make you free."* This is why I am excited for the opportunity to share some of these truths with you. I hope to be able to help you abide in His Word with this study tool. More than thirty years have passed, and I still have a stack of those original mini-books on my book shelf. I still value the experience I received from God through the study of His Word from those early days of my walk with Him.

I pray you will have a similar experience over the next one hundred days as you study these truths with me. May our good God bless you richly with revelation from His Word!

Born Again to Win,
Chaplain McComb

Part One:

THE FAITH LIFE

Introduction

The devotions in this section are on the topic of living by faith. Faith is a subject that is misunderstood and misapplied in our modern culture. Most people associate it as a belief system. For example, you hear people say, "What faith are you?" Meaning, "What religion are you?" or "What religious persuasion are you?" That isn't even close to the proper application of faith revealed in the Bible. Nor is faith something we use to try to get God to move or do something for us. Rather, faith is a positive response on your behalf to what God has already done. Faith is how you access God's grace to receive from Him.

I believe the devotions in this part of my devotional will help give you a better understanding of what faith is and some of the many areas of our Christianity that are involved. As you read, you will find each day's devotion deals with a different aspect of faith. I have included multiple scripture references within each devotion for you to use. If you will take a few minutes each day to read the devotion and then spend some time to meditate on each truth, pray, and look up the verses in your Bible, it will serve as a study guide to help you build your understanding of faith. I believe it will help build in you a revelation of this very important Bible subject we all need to major in. May our good God bless you and give you illumination as you read!

—Chaplain McComb

DAY 1

Children of God through Faith in Jesus

For you are all sons of God through faith in Christ Jesus.
For as many of you as were baptized into Christ have put
on Christ.

(Galatians 3:26–27)

While it is a fact all of humanity is a product of God's creation (Genesis 1:26–27), the Bible makes it clear in today's verse that mankind becomes *"sons of God through faith in Christ Jesus."* **Faith in Jesus**, that is, to believe He is Lord and the decision to act on the belief by confessing Jesus as your personal Lord and Savior (Romans 10:9–10) gives one the right to become a child of God, His sons and daughters!

John 1:12 tells us, *"But as many as received Him, to them He gave the right to become children of God, to those who believe in His name."* Becoming a child of God is not the privileged result of being born human. No, becoming children of God is a "right" bestowed upon those "who believe in His name"! It is a great honor to be a Christian, and every born-again believer has the

right to claim to be a "child of God"! This verse specifies this right is only extended to those who *"received Him"* by believing *"in His name"*.

We are told in today's verse (vs. 27) those who are *"baptized into Christ have put on Christ."* This is not describing water baptism. There is more than one baptism mentioned in Scripture. To be "baptized into Christ" is something which happens to every born-again believer immediately upon receiving salvation: *"For by one Spirit we were all baptized into one body..."* (1 Corinthians 12:13). We are placed (baptized) into the body of Christ at the new birth. As a member of the body of Christ, we are then adopted into God's family as sons/daughters (Galatians 4:5).

> *And because you are sons, God has sent forth the Spirit of His Son into your hearts, crying out, "Abba, Father!"*
> (Galatians 4:6)

One of the benefits of being God's son is receiving the indwelling of His Spirit. This allows the believer to address God in the same manner Jesus did, "Abba Father" (Mark 14:35–36), which carries the idea God is our Daddy. It is a term of affection and fondness! As God's adopted son/daughter, you have the right to His favor, blessing, provision, protection, and all the benefits of relationship as a natural child.

Father God, I believe as a child of God, it is my right and honor to relate to You as Your son/daughter.
Thank you...
Amen!

DAY 2

Faith is a Lifestyle

For I am not ashamed of the gospel of Christ, for it is the power of God to salvation for everyone who believes, for the Jew first and also for the Greek. For in it the righteousness of God is revealed from faith to faith; as it is written, "The just shall live by faith."

(Romans 1:16–17)

Notice the Apostle Paul said the "gospel of Christ" is the *"power of God to salvation."* **The gospel is the power of God** that releases the benefits of salvation into our lives. These benefits are received by putting faith in the gospel of Christ by acting on the belief that Jesus is Lord! The truths of the gospel are not clearly understood by many Christians. This is the reason why many are living below their rights and privileges, which are provided as benefits. They don't have the power of the gospel working in them.

Verse 17 ends with the words, *"The just shall live by faith."* This is a reference to Habakkuk 2:4, *"Behold the proud, His soul is not upright in him; But the just shall live by his faith."* Paul makes a very important point here, which is, faith is not something we use to be born again and forgiven of our sins then never to be used again. No, the just are to live by their faith! **Faith is to be a lifestyle for us!**

Romans 1:17 is a key verse to the entire Book of Romans. Understanding this truth of the just living by faith is key to understanding all the rest of the truth presented in Romans. As a matter of fact, Habakkuk 2:4 is referenced three times in the New Testament (Romans 1:17; Galatians 3:11; Hebrews 10:38)! Things are repeated in Scripture for the sake of emphasis.

You just can't over emphasize the importance of the Christian adopting this important lifestyle for their individual life. We are being instructed that the just **live** by faith. It is not something we try occasionally or use once a year if there is a need. No, living by faith should be at the forefront of our mind to be used in our daily walk with our God—something we use in relating to God in prayer, worship, receiving from God, and decisions we make in life.

Heavenly Father, I recognize the importance of living by faith. I will strengthen my faith in You by reading and applying the Word of God in my life.

Amen!

DAY 3

Justification by Faith in Jesus

But that no one is justified by the law in the sight of God is evident, for "the just shall live by faith."

(Galatians 3:11)

This is the second reference made by Paul in the New Testament to Habakkuk 2:4, *"...the just shall live by his faith."* The point being made here is **faith imparts spiritual life, not the works of the Law.** In this important Book of Galatians, Paul establishes the fact that the Law of Moses was only for a specific period of time. This is brought out clearly for us in Galatians 3:23, *"But before faith came, we were kept under guard by the law, kept for the faith which would afterward be revealed."* He is not referring to faith in general, such as the faith Abraham exercised before the Law. Rather, it is the faith described in verse 22, *"...faith in Jesus Christ..."*

The law acted as a barrier that prevented us from ever obtaining salvation by our own efforts or attempt at keeping the law perfectly. Verse 24 tells us the purpose the law served, *"Therefore the law was our tutor to bring us to Christ, that we might be justified by faith."* The law served as a disciplinarian only for a time until faith came, which would lead us into the freedom of full-grown sons no longer in need of a schoolmaster.

Romans 3:20 tells us, *"Therefore by the deeds of the law no flesh will be justified in His sight, for by the law is the knowledge of sin."* The law brought the knowledge of sin. It pointed out man's need for a savior. The law made everyone guilty and could not produce justification. The law drove everyone to attempt to keep a standard of holiness no one was capable of keeping.

It prepared us for the message of Christ, which brings salvation to us as a gift. Only to be received by **faith** in Jesus and what He has done for us. When God wanted to produce justification and righteousness in man, He did it through Jesus. Jesus brought a message of grace and truth (John 1:16–17), not law and wrath. **Faith in God's grace gift has now accomplished for us what the law never could!** There is now no need to strive for a perceived standard of perfection that produces a standing with our God! That barrier has been removed! *"But after faith has come, we are no longer under a tutor"* (Galatians 3:25).

Father, thank you for the free grace gift You have provided through faith in Jesus!
Amen!

DAY 4

Faith Believes and Speaks

And since we have the same spirit of faith, according to what is written, "I believed and therefore I spoke," we also believe and therefore speak.

(2 Corinthians 4:13)

In this verse, the Apostle Paul quotes the Old Testament psalmist, *"I believed and therefore I spoke..."* (Psalm 116:10). Notice he says we **have** the "same spirit of faith," not trying to have or hoping to obtain, or praying we can receive the same spirit of faith. No, we have it now, the same spirit of faith, which believes and speaks. This brings out an important, basic premise concerning the operation and effective use of our faith. Faith has two parts, believing in the heart and speaking with the mouth! Words are the "vehicle" that releases our faith. The words we speak are how we act on our faith.

This is seen clearly in Romans 10:9–10, *"that if you confess with your mouth the Lord Jesus and believe in your heart that God has raised Him from the dead, you will be saved. For with the heart one believes unto righteousness, and with the mouth confession is made unto salvation."* Our eternal salvation is not complete simply because we believe. Salvation is received by faith, which means we must believe and act on what we believe by confessing Jesus as Lord.

Believing in the heart and confessing with the mouth is essential to operating in faith. The point of origin for real Bible faith is the Word of God. Our believing must be based solidly on what God has spoken to us in the Bible. Our faith cannot be based on an experience we had or an experience someone else had, or something we were told. Ideally, those things would represent truth, but this is not always the case! Be certain you are believing the truth from the living Word of God! Truth is never established by an experience. Once the truth is known, it must be believed in the heart and confessed with the mouth to release the power of faith.

It matters what we believe, and we must guard our hearts with all diligence (Proverbs 4:23) because *"out of the abundance of the heart"* the *"mouth speaks"* (Luke 6:45). What you believe in your heart and speak from your mouth, your faith will empower to become a reality in your life!

Heavenly Father, I will guard my believing and speaking to operate in faith to receive from You.
Amen!

DAY 5

The Walk of Faith

For we walk by faith, not by sight.

(2 Corinthians 5:7)

This is a very important verse to be understood clearly in order to have an effective "faith life" and is key to developing the faith walk of the Christian life. We must learn to walk by faith rather than walking by sight. Most people get this exactly backward. Most people walk by sight rather than by faith. We are conditioned to believe what we see, taste, hear, smell, or feel. We often hear people say, "I'll believe it when I see it," but when it comes to the things of God, you are going to believe it before you see it, or you're not going to see it!

We are asked to believe in God and the things of God without seeing or experiencing physical evidence. This is a simple principle that is very difficult to do because most people are dominated by their senses. This is why the Bible instructs us to renew our minds,

And do not be conformed to this world, but be transformed by the renewing of your mind, that you may prove what is that good and acceptable and perfect will of God.

(Romans 12:2)

Faith sees and understands with the heart, "...*lest at any time they should see with their eyes and hear with their ears, and should understand with their heart...*" (Matthew 13:15 KJV). Faith is your positive response to what God has promised and done for us. In order to be acted upon, God's promises must be seen, heard, understood, and believed in the heart. There is a spiritual "seeing" which takes place in the heart (renewed mind and regenerated spirit), enabling one to act in pure faith to receive and manifest the promises of God offered by grace.

Part of the maturity process in our relationship with God is to come to the place where we no longer allow our mortal body to limit our walk with Him based upon our physical senses. As we hear the promises of the Word of God, faith is ignited within us (Romans 10:17) and then must be acted upon.

Acting upon the Word by the faith resident in the heart as opposed to walking according to the senses is the "walk of faith" as described in 2 Corinthians 5:7. Learn to make choices based upon the incorruptible seed of the Word (1 Peter 1:23) rather than your senses!

Heavenly Father, I make the decision today to walk by the Word and not by sight.

In Jesus' name...

Amen!

DAY 6

Faith Comes by Hearing

So then faith comes by hearing, and hearing by the word of God.

(Romans 10:17)

The only source for faith is hearing the Word of God from the Bible. People's testimonies can possibly be an encouragement, but they can also promote unbelief. Today's verse shows us our faith is built and ignited when we learn truth from the Word of God. Notice it does not say "faith comes by having heard". It is not okay to just rest on a revelation we learned from the past. No, we must continue *"by hearing, and hearing by the word of God."* Faith comes by hearing, and hearing, and hearing!

The more we hear the truth and assimilate it (believing it in our heart and speaking it), the more power is released. For example, it is not enough to believe God can heal. The average Christian believes God can do anything. But the average Christian also believes He has done nothing! The more we hear the truth preached concerning healing and what God has provided for us through Jesus' work, the more faith we develop to receive it for ourselves.

A great example of this is found in Paul's ministry, recorded in the Book of Acts. Paul was preaching the gospel at Lystra where a crippled man who had never walked was listening to the message: *"This man heard Paul speaking. Paul, observing him intently and seeing that he had faith to be healed..."* (Acts 14:9). As this man heard the Word of God's grace (Acts 14:3), it developed within him *"faith to be healed."* The next verse says Paul *"said with a loud voice, 'Stand up straight on your feet!' And he leaped and walked."*

This man was enabled to receive his miracle by the faith, which was ignited in his heart by hearing the truth! The same thing will happen for you if you will make an effort to hear the Word of God and then commit to continuing to feed yourself spiritually by hearing and hearing it again and again until it builds a developed faith in your heart!

As our minds are renewed (Romans 12:2), faith will replace unbelief which will enable us to receive from God the things offered by His grace. God is not withholding from you. He's offering all you need by His grace. We simply must learn how to receive it by faith!

Father, I am thankful for what You have done. I believe strong faith is building in me as I hear Your Word!

Amen!

DAY 7

Faith is the Evidence of Things Not Seen

Now faith is the substance of things hoped for, the evidence of things not seen. For by it the elders obtained a good testimony.

(Hebrews 11:1–2)

The author of the Book of Hebrews made an important point in this verse to help us understand what faith is. First notice verse 2 says, *"For by it the elders obtained a good testimony."* The understood subject of the sentence is faith. The word "elders" is a reference to Old Testament saints. Did you know the Old Testament saints lived by faith? Faith has always been the way man has approached God and will always be the way man approaches God! So, it is imperative to know what it is!

There is a distinct difference between faith and hope. Faith is not hope, and hope is not faith. You can hope for something and exercise no faith. Hope is not a bad thing, but you must know the difference between faith and hope. Hope is a good goal setter, but it will not access the grace of God for you. For example, *"And the prayer of faith will save the sick, and the Lord will raise him up..."* (James 5:15).

It's not hope which will save the sick; it is the prayer of faith. Hope is always future tense; faith is present tense. In other words, you must believe you receive it **now**, when you pray it, not hoping to get it someday. If you are just wishing and hoping, you aren't in faith.

Faith is not a blind leap into the unknown. Faith is a calculated step that rests assuredly on the promises of God! Faith is evidence. In a court of law, evidence becomes proof. Evidence isn't the act; evidence just proves the act occurred. Faith, based on God's Word, is all the proof we need; it's the evidence of things not seen. I wasn't there to see Jesus on the cross or the whipping post, but by faith, I am rock solid that it occurred! Many want to see it before they believe it (see Day 5 devotion), but for the Christian, faith is the evidence of that which is not seen.

We have to go beyond hoping life will get better for us. We have to exercise faith to approach God and receive from Him—faith in the truth and the value of that which is promised us in the Bible!

Heavenly Father, by faith, Your Word is all the evidence I need.
I believe in Jesus' name...
Amen!

DAY 8

Mustard Seed Faith

So Jesus said to them, "Because of your unbelief; for assuredly, I say to you, if you have faith as a mustard seed, you will say to this mountain, 'Move from here to there,' and it will move; and nothing will be impossible for you."

(Matthew 17:20)

Matthew 17 records for us the story of Jesus being transfigured before Peter, James, and John on the mount (Matthew 17:1–13). When they came down from the mountain, they found a man had brought his epileptic son to the disciples to be healed (vs. 15–16). Jesus' disciples ministered to the boy but were unable to help him. Jesus was not pleased with their inability to help the boy. He said they were *"faithless and perverse"* (vs. 17). The reason He was displeased is that He had already authorized them and empowered them to do it (Matthew 10:7–8), but they didn't do it!

Jesus was not okay with their inability to help the boy. If you don't think so, why did He rebuke them so severely? Most people would think, "At least they tried," and think no more of it because they are mere men. That's not the way Jesus thought about it. He expected them to use their faith to bring the power of God into the situation to heal and deliver! When the disciples asked why they were unable to cast the demon out of the boy, verse 20 (quoted above) was His response.

The reason was because of their unbelief. Most people don't think of it this way. Most would consider it a lack of faith. It doesn't take huge faith to move your mountain, just pure faith—faith that is not contaminated with unbelief. If you will remove the unbelief, you will find your faith is powerful enough to move the mountain out of your life! People who tolerate huge amounts of unbelief are not able to overcome the unbelief and assume they don't have faith. We don't need more faith. Jesus said **it only takes *"faith as a mustard seed"* to move the mountain.** What we need is less unbelief!

Know this today, faith is powerful and will receive from God for you if it is not contaminated with doubt, fear, or unbelief. If you will remove the contaminants, you will find more success in prayer and receiving the promises in your life! God does expect us to cooperate with Him by faith!

Father, I believe faith is powerful to remove mountains. I am committed to receive by faith!

Amen!

DAY 9

Faith Pleases God

But without faith it is impossible to please Him, for he who comes to God must believe that He is, and that He is a rewarder of those who diligently seek Him.

(Hebrews 11:6)

What an important verse this is to help us understand what pleases God! As a prison Chaplain, I regularly encounter men who carry shame and guilt for the things they have done. Because of their "performance mentality," they think God could not accept them or be pleased with them. I think we all can understand how we have developed this type of thinking.

I wasn't raised in your home, but I was raised in an American home. When we did well, what happened? We were rewarded. When we performed poorly, what happened? We were punished. As a result, we develop the mentality, "Do good, get good". If we perform well, we expect to be accepted and rewarded, but if we are bad, we expect punishment or rejection. As a result, we carry this "performance mentality" into our relationship with God thinking, *Do good, get good.*

God is not relating to you based on your performance! **God is relating to you based on your faith in Jesus' performance!** Your faith is accounted to you as righteousness (Romans 3:21–22). It pleases God when you make the choice to place faith in what Jesus has done to put you in right standing and justification before God (Romans 5:1).

You could never do enough good works to be good enough to please God. Reading your Bible, prayer, and church attendance can never be enough to earn standing with God. Someone may say, "Wait a minute, preacher! Are you saying we don't need to do those things?" No, I think you should read your Bible, pray, and go to church, but I do not think you should do any of those things to try to please God!

You cannot **"do"** enough to please Him! What does please Him is simple faith in the gospel of Jesus Christ. As a Christian, we should want to worship God, serve others, and do good works to be a blessing. Just don't develop the attitude that your service is being done to please God. Nor should we develop the attitude when we fail or make mistakes that God no longer loves us or is displeased with us. **If you're placing faith in God, He's more pleased with you than you know.**

Father, I'm glad to know You are pleased with me because of my faith.

Thank you...

Amen!

DAY 10

Faith is the Victory

For whatever is born of God overcomes the world. And this is the victory that has overcome the world—our faith.

(1 John 5:4)

The Apostle John made it clear in this verse it is God's plan for those who are born again to overcome the world. Christians are not supposed to be beaten down and defeated. That is not a good testimony of what our God has done! The Apostle Paul said very much the same under the inspiration of the Holy Spirit. He said tribulation, distress, persecution, famine, nakedness, peril, or the sword could not separate us from the love of Christ.

Yet in all these things we are more than conquerors through Him who loved us.

(Romans 8:37)

A conqueror has the victory and the spoils of war, but he has to fight to get them. We are more than conquerors because **we have the victory and all the spoils, but we didn't have to fight**

to get them. Jesus did the fighting for us! This is important for you to understand. We are not headed toward a victory. **We are coming from a victory!** The victory was won for us by Jesus at the cross. Now, all we have to do is receive the benefits by faith.

One of the greatest lessons you can learn about faith is, faith is not something you use to try to get God to do something for you. Faith is not something you use to try to get God to move. People who do not understand this approach God as beggars trying to get Him to move. God has already moved. Jesus has won the victory and has made it all available to us. All we have to do is receive by faith. We are to enforce the victory which has already been won, using the faith and authority given to us by our God.

Always approach the devil and your problems from this perspective. You are an overcomer and more than a conqueror. You do not have to win the war; the war has already been won. As one who is born of God, know victory has been won! Faith doesn't give you the victory; no, faith is the victory! Victory is yours, but it has to be appropriated, in other words, taken for your own use! Cooperate with God by using your faith to rise above the circumstances and enforce the victory which is yours.

Heavenly Father, thank you for the victory Jesus won for me. I believe I walk in victory by faith!
Amen!

DAY 11

Justified by Faith

But to him who does not work but believes on Him who justifies the ungodly, his faith is accounted for righteousness.

(Romans 4:5)

God justifies the ungodly. When you read that statement, it has one of two effects on you; it either really blesses you or really offends you. Those who believe we must earn our standing with God through good works and holy living would take offense at the statement. But those of us who believe faith without works is righteousness, love and understand that statement. Let's read today's verse again, *"But to him who does not work but believes on Him who justifies the ungodly, his faith is accounted for righteousness."* There it is, straight from the Bible! If you didn't see it for yourself, you might be tempted to believe it isn't there.

In Romans, Chapter 4, the Apostle Paul is making the point Abraham was justified by faith apart from his performance (keeping the law). Paul was countering the false doctrine that our actions, or our good performance, will produce righteousness with God. He then makes the point even David described this blessedness and then referenced Psalm 32:1–2.

Blessed is he whose transgression is forgiven, Whose sin is covered. Blessed is the man to whom the Lord does not impute iniquity. And in whose spirit there is no deceit.

(Psalm 32:1–2)

Blessed are those whose lawless deeds are forgiven, And whose sins are covered; Blessed is the man to whom the Lord shall not impute sin.

(Romans 4:7–8)

Notice it doesn't say, God did not or God does not impute sin. No, it says God *"shall not impute sin"* against us! Wow! This means all of our sins have been dealt with, past, present, and future. God will never in the future hold our sins against us! As believers, our sins were imputed to Jesus, and justification was imputed to us! God dealt with Jesus according to our sin, so remission of sin can come to us. **This is important because those who think they still have to pay for their sins dishonor Jesus!** Furthermore, those who don't believe they have been justified by faith in what He has done for us dishonor Jesus!

It's important we understand this, so our conscience doesn't condemn us. All of us have made mistakes and done things we shouldn't have, but know this today; **God justifies the ungodly through faith in Jesus and what He has done for us!** It will enable you to enjoy your relationship with God without shame and fear of condemnation!

Father God, thank you that through Jesus, I have been made righteous in Your eyes.
Amen!

DAY 12

Saved through Faith

For by grace you have been saved through faith, and that not of yourselves; it is the gift of God, not of works, lest anyone should boast.

(Ephesians 2:8-9)

This verse gives us some very important information about how salvation is offered to us and how we are to receive it. Salvation is not given as a sovereign choice of God. No, salvation is offered as a whosoever will proposition (Romans 10:13)—notice we are not saved by grace alone. **We are saved by grace *through* faith.** Salvation is freely offered by God's grace to everyone, but it must be received by faith.

The basic premise in everything God has provided for us is, **what God offers by grace must be received by faith!** Faith gives us access into God's grace (Romans 5:2). Without faith, God's grace is wasted. Without grace, faith is powerless. Grace is God's part. If God is not offering it by grace, you can't get it by faith. He now offers everything Christ has provided for us by grace, but it is not automatic.

Titus 2:11 says, *"For the grace of God that brings salvation has appeared to all men."* Salvation is offered as a gift to all mankind, but not all men are saved because not all receive the gift by faith. Failure to understand the role of both faith and grace has led to much confusion in the body of Christ. Some emphasize the grace of God to such an extreme that everything is up to the sovereignty of God. This makes faith useless. They say everything is up to God alone, which is wrong. Others emphasize faith apart from grace which leads to legalism. Both extreme viewpoints are incorrect! We need a balanced view of the role of both grace and faith to receive from God. Grace is God's part; faith is man's part.

Salvation is being described as a gift. A gift is offered freely without any compensation provided to receive it. This is brought out clearly in Ephesians 2:8–9, "...*it is the gift of God, not of works, lest anyone should boast.*" The only acceptable response to salvation is gratitude and praise to God for His indescribable gift (2 Corinthians 9:15). Salvation is a gift to be received, not a wage to be earned (Romans 6:23). Know today this gift is offered to us freely without any trust in our own good works or effort to earn it.

Father, I thank you for the free gift of salvation offered by Your grace.
I receive it by faith in Jesus' name...
Amen!

DAY 13

Faith in the Name

And His name, through faith in His name, has made this man strong, whom you see and know. Yes, the faith which comes through Him has given him this perfect soundness in the presence of you all.

(Acts 3:16)

This familiar story from Acts, Chapter 3, beautifully illustrates for us the power in the name of Jesus. As Peter and John went to the Jewish temple to pray, they encountered a lame beggar at the gate. When the apostles approached him, he asked them for alms (Acts 3:1–5). Peter's response to him was,

Silver and gold I do not have, but what I do have I give you: In the name of Jesus Christ of Nazareth, rise up and walk.

(Acts 3:6)

Peter knew he had something to give this man! Peter used the name of Jesus to minister healing to him! *"And he took him by the right hand and lifted him up, and immediately his feet and ankle bones received strength. So he, leaping up, stood and walked and entered the temple with them—walking, leaping, and praising God"*

(Acts 3:7–8). It says the man leaped up! This has to be interpreted as faith on his part.

This brings out an important point to be understood. **Faith has to be present for miracles to happen!** It needs to be present either in the minister, the one being ministered to, or a corporate faith among those present, for the power of God to manifest this way.

The healed man held on to Peter as he was learning to walk and went into the temple, where the people were amazed at this notable miracle. At that time, Peter began to preach his second sermon and made the amazing statement in verse 16 (quoted above), *"His name, through **faith in His name**, has made this man strong..."* (emphasis mine). Peter's words make it clear this wasn't just a sovereign choice of God to heal this man. No, the two men cooperated with God by placing faith in the name of Jesus to manifest this healing miracle!

> *Therefore God also has highly exalted Him and given Him the name which is above every name.*
>
> (Philippians 2:9)

The name of Jesus is powerful and has been given to the Church to use (Mark 16:15–18). As a believer, you have been authorized by Jesus to use His name in prayer, to receive healing and deliverance, and make disciples.

Heavenly Father, I'm thankful You have given me the strong name of Jesus. I have faith in the name today!
In Jesus' name...
Amen!

DAY 14

Gentiles Are Justified by Faith

Therefore know that only those who are of faith are sons of Abraham. And the Scripture, foreseeing that God would justify the Gentiles by faith, preached the gospel to Abraham beforehand, saying, "In you all the nations shall be blessed."

(Galatians 3:7–8)

Over and over in the New Testament, Abraham is referred to as an example of faith at work and even as the father of us all. *"Therefore it is of faith that it might be according to grace, so that the promise might be sure to all the seed, not only to those who are of the law, but also to those who are of the faith of Abraham, who is the father of us all"* (Romans 4:16). So, there is much for us to learn from his life.

Just as it is our faith, which makes us pleasing to God (Hebrews 11:6), Abraham's faith was pleasing to God. It certainly wasn't his performance or genealogy. But the Jews missed that point. They mistakenly believed it was the physical descendants who would be the heirs of Abraham's blessings and God's covenant. Paul corrected that with his interpretation of Genesis 12:3, "...*And in you all the families of the earth shall be blessed.*" He makes the point everyone who puts faith in Christ is a true child of Abraham, whether Jew or Gentile.

The fact that all nations would be blessed through him meant Gentiles would be saved without becoming Jews. **This foretold salvation by grace rather than by the works of the law.** The way Abraham received his blessing was by faith, and this is the way the New Testament Christian will receive them as well. The whole point of the Galatian letter is there is no requirement for Gentile Christians to go back under the law and live as Jews (Galatians 2:14).

There are things we can learn from the law but know this...

> *But before faith came, we were kept under guard by the law, kept for the faith which would afterward be revealed. Therefore the law was our tutor to bring us to Christ, that we might be justified by faith. But after faith has come, we are no longer under a tutor.*
>
> (Galatians 3:23–25)

Be careful you are building your doctrinal understanding according to the New Testament revelation of truth. **In these days we are living in, we relate to God strictly by our faith** in Him and His Word!

Father, I am thankful we are no longer under the law to serve You. I believe I am blessed by faith.

Amen!

DAY 15

Effective Sharing of Your Faith

That the sharing of your faith may become effective by the acknowledgment of every good thing which is in you in Christ Jesus.

(Philemon 1:6)

Every born-again believer has been given the measure of faith (Romans 12:3), so possession of faith is not an issue. We have faith (2 Corinthians 4:13); there is no need to beg God for faith or try to obtain it another way. We simply need to develop the faith we already have and learn to use it in our lives. This is what today's verse is addressing. It says the *"sharing of your faith"* becomes effective. The word "sharing" has to do with the release or use of our faith.

It then tells us our faith becomes effective *"by the acknowledgment of every good thing"* which is in us. **We are supposed to acknowledge the good things which are in us** because we are in Christ. Many Christians are not aware of the many "in-Christ realities" which are ours. As a result, they tend to believe there is nothing good in us, and they quote the Apostle Paul as a basis for this belief.

Paul did say in Romans 7:18, *"For I know that in me (that is, in my flesh) nothing good dwells; for to will is present with me, but how to perform what is good I do not find."* The important thing to notice about this is the parenthetical phrase "that is, in my flesh". He was saying, apart from Christ there was no good thing in him, but he was not apart from Christ. If you are born again, you are not apart from Christ either! If you do not acknowledge the many wonderful things resident in your spirit, your faith will be hindered!

As we begin to understand, by the renewing of our mind (Romans 12:2), what has been done for us and been given to us, the effectiveness of our faith will increase. It is important to acknowledge we have faith (2 Corinthians 4:13), we are the righteousness of God in Christ (2 Corinthians 5:21), we are blessed with all spiritual blessings in Christ (Ephesians 1:3), etc. The Apostle John said in 3 John 1:2, *"Beloved, I pray that you may prosper in all things and be in health, just as your soul prospers."* We can expect to prosper and be in health according to the degree we prosper our souls!

Father, I want to acknowledge all the good things You have done for me and in me.

Thank you, in Jesus' name...
Amen!

DAY 16

Faith is Voice Activated

So Jesus answered and said to them, "Have faith in God."
(Mark 11:22)

Mark, Chapter 11, records for us the activity that took place during the final week of Jesus' life before His crucifixion. During that week, Jesus and the apostles would spend the night in Bethany about two miles from Jerusalem. On the second day walking into Jerusalem, Jesus was hungry, *"And seeing from afar a fig tree having leaves, He went to see if perhaps He would find something on it. When He came to it, He found nothing but leaves, for it was not the season for figs. In response Jesus said to it, 'Let no one eat fruit from you ever again.' And His disciples heard it"* (Mark 11:13–14). Jesus spoke to this tree! It wasn't a silent request. Jesus didn't ask God to kill the tree. He spoke to the tree out loud, then walked on into town.

The next day, as they passed it again, they found it dried up from the roots. *"And Peter, remembering, said to Him, 'Rabbi, look! The fig tree which You cursed has withered away'"* (Mark 11:21). Jesus then used this as an object lesson to teach them how faith works, *"Have faith in God"* (vs. 22).

He continued in verse 23, *"For assuredly, I say to you, whoever says to this mountain, 'Be removed and be cast into the sea,' and does not doubt in his heart, but believes that those things he says will be done, he will have whatever he says."* We are told by Jesus to speak to the mountain. Most people want to speak to God about their mountain, but that is not what Jesus said!

Faith is released by speaking words. **We are commanded to believe in the power of our words** and that they will come to pass! Faith is voice activated. If we refuse this lesson and instead speak words of doubt and believe those words in our hearts, we will eventually receive those results in our life.

When a problem stands against us, **we are to speak to the problem** (mountain) and believe we have what we say. Proverbs 18:21 says, *"Death and life are in the power of the tongue, and those who love it will eat its fruit."* Your words are releasing either death or life into your situation. Faith for victory is released as you speak your words!

Father, I believe in the power of my words. I believe my faith is activating Your power in my life.

Amen!

DAY 17

The Prayer of Faith

So Jesus answered and said to them, "Have faith in God.
Therefore I say to you, whatever things you ask when you
pray, believe that you receive them, and you will have them."
(Mark 11:22, 24)

This is a continuation of Jesus' lesson on faith from the cursing of the fig tree. Jesus used it as an object lesson to teach on the power of, and the operation of, our faith. Verse 24 is dealing specifically with the prayer of faith in regard to the things we ask God for, *"whatever things you ask when you pray."*

Now notice the qualification Jesus placed upon this type of prayer, *"believe that you receive them, and you will have them."* We are commanded by our Lord to believe we receive the answers to our prayer when we pray them! This means we must believe God hears and answers as we are praying. The prayer of faith believes it receives and expects it to come to pass **when you pray!**

The believing which is required "when you pray" is to be done while the thing you desired is still yet to come to pass. This may only take an instant or longer to come to pass, but Jesus said, "you will have them." God moves instantly to answer our prayers which meet His qualifications such as **asking according to His will** (1 John 5:14–15), **asking in faith** (Matthew 21:22), **asking without wavering** (James 1:5–7), and **not consuming it upon our own lusts** (James 4:2–3), etc. And when the qualifications according to His Word are met, God answers!

Although God answers right away, because He moves in the spiritual realm, His workings are not immediately evident to our physical senses. By faith, we must believe He is answering our prayers even before we see physical evidence. If we fail to believe, that is doubt which will prevent us from receiving. Jesus said, *"For everyone who asks receives, and he who seeks finds, and to him who knocks it will be opened"* (Matthew 7:8). This must always be the basic premise of our prayers, that God is inclined to answer us and everyone who asks receives!

God is not withholding from us. He desires to answer our prayers. Our part is to meet the scriptural requirements for prayer, to know the will of God, expect it to come to pass, and know God answers!

Father, I believe You desire to answer my prayers. I will cooperate with You in the prayer of faith, in Jesus' name...

Amen!

DAY 18

We Access God's Grace by Faith

Through whom also we have access by faith into this grace
in which we stand, and rejoice in hope of the glory of God.

(Romans 5:2)

Notice the Apostle Paul stated in this verse, we stand in grace. This is most important for us to understand. In Romans, Chapter 4, Paul made the point Abraham was justified by faith alone, not through any works or keeping of the Law of Moses. We are justified the same way. God is dealing with us strictly by grace!

In this Church age we are living in, God is dealing with man according to His grace. Salvation is offered by grace; forgiveness is offered by grace, healing, deliverance, anything you want to name. If you are going to get something from God, it is going to be received by faith through His grace (Titus 2:11; Ephesians 2:8).

Grace is God's part; faith is our part. You could think of it like this; grace is God reaching down to man. It is God-given ability on our behalf, undeserved and unearned. This is where the idea of "unmerited favor" originated. There is not anything we can do to earn it; it is freely given by God. Grace is God powerfully doing for man what man cannot do for himself.

Faith is man reaching up to God. By faith, we access the grace of God! The word "access" in Romans 5:2 is translated from a Greek word which literally means "admission".[1] When you go to the movie theater, you must purchase a ticket to be granted admission. Your ticket then allows you access to the movie being shown. In much the same way, think of your faith (believing and speaking, 2 Corinthians 4:13) as the ticket that grants admission into God's grace. Your faith accesses the grace of God to enable you to receive from Him. **Everything He has provided is now offered by grace, but it must be received by faith.**

God does not work in your life independent of you. He works in you through you. Which means you must cooperate with Him by exercising faith to receive. God has blessed us with every spiritual blessing (Ephesians 1:3), which is now offered to us by grace. When you understand this, you can *rejoice in hope of the glory of God."*

Father, I am so thankful You relate to me by grace. I believe You offer everything I need by grace, and I receive it by faith.

In Jesus' name...

Amen!

---

1 "Strong's Greek: 4318," (Bible Hub, 2021), https://biblehub.com/greek/4318.htm.

DAY 19

The Shield of Faith

Above all, taking the shield of faith with which you will be able to quench all the fiery darts of the wicked one.

(Ephesians 6:16)

In Ephesians, Chapter 6, we are instructed to put on the whole armor of God (vs. 11). The reason is that we are in a spiritual war. Like it or not, there is a war in the spiritual realm for the spirit and soul of every human. We have much to do with the outcome of the war in our individual lives. We must understand Satan has been totally defeated by Jesus on the cross. Always deal with the devil from the perspective he is a defeated foe! **We do not need to defeat the devil, but we do need to enforce the victory.**

We are provided the armor of God because of the ongoing spiritual battles. Physical weapons are useless in spiritual matters. We must have God's armor to defend ourselves. All of the listed weapons (Ephesians 6:10–18) are important for us, but we are told, *"Above all, talking the shield of faith..."* (vs. 16). The words "above all" mean overall and in front of all. The armor being described in this chapter is likened to the Roman soldier's armor of Paul's day. They carried a shield as a defensive weapon and stationed it in front of them to protect them from the fiery arrows fired by their enemy.

Likewise, we are told the shield of faith will *"...be able to quench all the fiery darts of the wicked one"* (Ephesians 6:16). One of the strategies of our enemy in this war is to hurl "fiery darts" of accusation against us continually. One of the names of Satan is the *accuser of the brethren* (Revelation 12:10–11). He will attack our sense of righteousness, our relationship with God, and tempt us to draw back from God. With our shield firmly in place, it will quench every attack!

Satan will shoot his fiery darts, but victory is possible in this life. *"Now thanks be to God who always leads us in triumph in Christ..."* (2 Corinthians 2:14). God wants you to win in life, and He has provided the armor to help you. Keep your faith strong by feeding it on the Word of God (Romans 10:17). Your revelation of this truth will keep your shield firmly in place in front of you to protect you!

Father, I believe You want me to win and have provided armor to help me. Thank you for the shield of faith.

Amen!

DAY 20

Faith in the Authority of the Spoken Word

When Jesus heard it, He marveled, and said to those who followed, "Assuredly, I say to you, I have not found such great faith, not even in Israel!"

(Matthew 8:10)

Notice this verse says Jesus marveled at the Centurion's great faith! This is one of only two times in all of Scripture where Jesus marveled. The other time was when He marveled at the Jews' unbelief in His own hometown of Nazareth (Mark 6:6). This is important enough that it is worth studying. We're told Jesus entered into Capernaum and a Roman Centurion came to Him pleading with Him about his paralyzed servant at home who was "*dreadfully tormented*" (vs. 6).

There was no hesitation on Jesus' part, "*And Jesus said to him, 'I will come and heal him'*" (vs. 7). Jesus was willing to go with the man to heal his servant, but the man stopped Him because he felt unworthy. He then asked Jesus to just "*speak a word, and my servant will be healed*" (vs. 8). He then began to explain his understanding of authority. This was a Gentile in the Roman military with command of one hundred troops. As a Centurion he had authority to command troops and they would obey (vs. 9).

He believed Jesus had the authority to speak the Word, and the servant would be healed! It was this man's understanding of authority that caused Jesus to marvel and call it great faith! He didn't need Jesus to come to his house because he had faith in Jesus' spoken Word! This is a great lesson for us. The Word of God, spoken in faith, can do all that the person of Jesus can do! **The faith which caused Jesus to marvel was faith in the authority of the spoken Word!**

Jesus had not found this kind of understanding even among the Jews in Israel. *"Then Jesus said to the centurion, 'Go your way; and as you have believed, so let it be done for you.' And his servant was healed that same hour"* (vs. 13). Notice it was the man's cooperation with Jesus which enabled the miracle to come to pass. Jesus told him, *"as you have believed, so let it be done for you."* **The servant was healed the very same hour his master believed the spoken Word!** Even though Jesus was not physically present, healing manifested in the servant. You can access God's power as well by believing the spoken Word.

Heavenly Father, I believe Your power is released as I speak Your Word in Faith!

In Jesus' name...

Amen!

DAY 21

Faith for Everyday Issues

And the apostles said to the Lord, "Increase our faith."

(Luke 17:5)

Sometimes people have the idea they don't have enough faith or possibly need extra faith to receive something "big" from God. There was a time when Jesus' own ministry team felt the same way. This is described for us in Luke, *"Take heed to your-selves. If your brother sins against you, rebuke him; and if he repents, forgive him. And if he sins against you seven times in a day, and seven times in a day returns to you, saying, 'I repent,' you shall forgive him"* (Luke 17:3-4). They were probably overwhelmed at the thought of forgiving the same person seven times in one day! Their response was *"Increase our faith"*! (vs. 5).

Jesus had been performing miracles, signs, and wonders, the kind of which they had never seen before. His men observed it all, but it wasn't the supernatural power display that prompted them to make their request. It was when Jesus spoke to them about forgiving someone seven times in a single day that prompted them to make their request "Increase our faith"!

There is a very important lesson to be learned from this. **Our faith isn't just for the miraculous.** It shouldn't be reserved for use only for the big issues in our lives. No, **our faith is for everyday issues** as well. We should use our faith to help us love people who have hurt us or offended us. We should use our faith at home in dealing with family issues or at work dealing with stress or people problems we encounter. We should use our faith to display the fruit of the Spirit in our lives daily, expressing love, joy, peace, longsuffering, kindness, goodness, faithfulness, gentleness, and self-control! (Galatians 5:22–23).

We can use our faith to overcome temptation, habits, and addictions and to build strong character in our lives. Faith isn't only for the situations we face which seem impossible; it is for the little things in life as well—some of which aren't so little!

This is something that will help us be more victorious in life. I can tell you, God does want us to be able to overcome those things in life which steal our joy, or our peace, or the things that hinder us from displaying fruit in our lives that will honor Him. I hope this encourages you to use your faith in this way!

Father, please help me to use my faith for the everyday issues in my life.

Amen!

DAY 22

The Fight of Faith

Fight the good fight of faith, lay hold on eternal life, to which you were also called and have confessed the good confession in the presence of many witnesses.

(1 Timothy 6:12)

It is important to understand the *"fight of faith"* mentioned in this verse. As I have emphasized previously, in several articles, we understand the devil has already been defeated by Jesus on the cross. Our "fight" does not mean we must defeat him. **There is a struggle in the Christian life, but the struggle isn't with God.** The struggle is with ourselves and the devil's lies. The struggle with ourselves is the constant need to resist the desires of the flesh, *"Therefore put to death your members which are on the earth: fornication, uncleanness, passion, evil desire, and covetousness, which is idolatry"* (Colossians 3:5). We are instructed to resist the devil as well, *"Therefore submit to God. Resist the devil and he will flee from you"* (James 4:7). No Christian is exempt from this fight. Those who refuse to fight...lose.

The New Testament was written originally in the Greek language. The word used for "fight" in verse 12 (quoted above) means "to struggle, to compete for a prize, or to contend with an adversary".[2] There are some people who don't want to fight. They are only interested in that which comes effortlessly. They might argue that the will of God is automatic. We hear it a lot among Christians. They say things like, "Everything happens for a reason," or "If it is meant to be, it will be." The thinking is, God is in control, and whatever He wants to be done gets done. If you will think for just a moment, though, you will have to acknowledge not everything God wants to be done is being accomplished. There are plenty of things happening in this world that God didn't want to be done. Thus, the reason we are told to submit to God and then resist the devil!

Notice verse 12 (quoted above) tells us to *lay hold on eternal life.*" God has given us eternal life by His grace, but after receiving salvation, we must put forth some effort to *"lay hold*" of it now to reap the benefits. Some people believe all of the benefits of our salvation are in eternity. But God wants us to enjoy life now! (Galatians 1:4). Thus, the reason to "fight" and "lay hold" in our Christian walk!

Father, I am thankful for what You have given me. And I will fight the good fight of faith.

Amen!

---

2 "Greek: *Agonizomai,*" Online Bible Commentary - Andrew Wommack Ministries (2021), https://www.awmi.net/reading/online-bible-commentary/?bn=1-timothy&cn=6&vn=12.

DAY 23

The Measure of Faith

For I say, through the grace given to me, to everyone who is among you, not to think of himself more highly than he ought to think, but to think soberly, as God has dealt to each one a measure of faith.

(Romans 12:3)

The Book of Romans was written by the Apostle Paul and addressed to the believers in Rome (Romans 1:7). Notice today's verse says, *"to everyone who is among you."* So, this verse is dealing with believers, applicable to the entire Church today. The verse concludes with the phrase *"as God has dealt to each one a measure of faith."* This means every believer has been given a measure of faith!

The biggest lie of the devil is, and you may have heard him say it to you, "You just don't have faith!" It is not true you do not have faith. If you are a Christian, you have faith. You can't even be saved without it! It may be true you have not developed your faith, you may not use your faith, or you may not understand it, but it is not true that you don't have faith!

You do not have to ask God to give you faith, or try to earn it through fasting and prayer, etc. God has given you a measure of faith; you just have to develop it and cause it to grow. You can develop your faith by doing two things:

1. Exercise it by putting it into practice.
2. Feed it on the Word of God.

If you will do these two things, your faith will begin to develop and become strong.

Everyone reading this understands you develop muscle by exercising. We all have muscles, which are developed through use, either in a weight room or another form of exercise. Our muscles become strong through use. The same is true about faith. The more we use our faith, the stronger it becomes.

The second thing to do is feed it on the Word of God (see Romans 10:17, Day 6). Any dietician will tell you these two basic premises are essential for good body health. The same is true for your faith/spirituality. Faith will be continually developed over the course of your lifetime. If you will commit to doing these two things, you will become strong and prove the will of God in your life!

Father, I thank you that You have given me faith. I'm committed to developing it to become strong.

Amen!

DAY 24

Let Christ Live in You by Faith

I have been crucified with Christ; it is no longer I who live, but Christ lives in me; and the life which I now live in the flesh I live by faith in the Son of God, who loved me and gave Himself for me.

(Galatians 2:20)

Paul was preaching death to self, but it is important to understand how this death took place. Paul was dead through what Jesus did. *"Knowing this, that our old man was crucified with Him, that the body of sin might be done away with, that we should no longer be slaves of sin"* (Romans 6:6). Walking in resurrection power in our physical life is dependent upon knowing our old man is crucified. If you don't believe that, there won't be a newness of life.

Therefore we were buried with Him through baptism into death, that just as Christ was raised from the dead by the glory of the Father, even so we also should walk in newness of life.

(Romans 6:4)

There is a common belief that our old man (sin nature) is still alive, and there is a fight on the inside of us between our old man and our new man, like two mad dogs in a fight within us driving us in a certain direction. People experience a drive to sin and assume it is their old sin nature driving them to it. Scripture does teach everyone was born with a sin nature, but Paul is making it very clear in these verses the sin nature/old man is dead! It is not the old nature compelling us; it is the lingering effects the old nature left behind in our flesh in the form of bad habits, addictions, and strongholds in our thoughts and emotions, which is why we are to bring every thought captive! (2 Corinthians 10:3–5).

The reason Christians sin is because of an un-renewed mind, not the sin nature. As we renew our minds to these truths and build faith in us by hearing the Word of God (Romans 10:17), we become formed in Christ's image (Romans 8:29; Colossians 1:27). The challenge before us all now is to let Christ live in us by faith in the Son of God!

There is no longer a part of me which is a sinner by nature, or you either if you are a Christian (2 Corinthians 5:17). Use your faith to let the life of Christ flow through you.

Father, I live by faith in the Son of God. I pray that Christ and His life will flow through me.

Amen!

DAY 25

Sanctified by Faith

To open their eyes, in order to turn them from darkness to light, and from the power of Satan to God, that they may receive forgiveness of sins and an inheritance among those who are sanctified by faith in Me.

(Acts 26:18)

Paul's return to Jerusalem after his missionary journeys and before his pending arrest is recorded in Acts, Chapter 21. The following chapters record his defense to the Jewish leadership, Felix the procurator (governor) of Judaea, and after appealing to Caesar, on to King Agrippa. While presenting his case to Agrippa, he recounts his experience with Jesus on the road to Damascus (Acts 9:3–6), where Jesus revealed to him that he was being called to minister to the Gentiles.

Acts 26:18 (quoted above) was the message he was to take to the Gentiles. Jesus told him His message to them was they were being allowed to turn to God, receive forgiveness of sins, and an inheritance *"among those who are sanctified by faith in Me."* The word "sanctified" means to "purify" or "consecrate".[3] Notice, they would be "sanctified by **faith**."

3 "Strong's Greek: G37 – Sanctified," (King James Bible Dictionary, 2021), http://kingjamesbibledictionary.com/StrongsNo/G37/sanctified.

The doctrine of sanctification has to do with the renewal of the fallen nature, cleansing of sin, and setting apart unto God. The way this happens is through faith in Jesus! It is not through any good works we have done or could do. There were many forms of worship as well as many false gods the Gentile world was accustomed to. An example is found in Acts 17:22–23,

> Then Paul stood in the midst of the Areopagus and said, "Men of Athens, I perceive that in all things you are very religious; for as I was passing through and considering the objects of your worship, I even found an altar with this inscription: TO THE UNKNOWN GOD. Therefore, the One whom you worship without knowing, Him I proclaim to you."

Although they were *"very religious,"* their religion was unable to sanctify them in the sight of God. It's not through religious efforts or holy living which will produce genuine cleansing and setting apart unto God that He desires. Although many are sincere, they are sincerely wrong. The true cleansing and setting apart of a sanctified vessel is only attained one way, through genuine faith in Jesus Christ and His redemptive work! Paul told the Philippian (Gentile) jailer precisely how to be saved/sanctified,

> Believe on the Lord Jesus Christ, and you will be saved, you and your household.

> (Acts 16:31)

Father, I believe I am sanctified by faith in Jesus' redemptive work. Thank you for cleansing me and setting me apart unto Yourself. Amen!

DAY 26

Established in Faith

As you therefore have received Christ Jesus the Lord, so walk in Him, rooted and built up in Him and established in the faith, as you have been taught, abounding in it with thanksgiving.

(Colossians 2:6–7)

In today's verse, the Apostle Paul is making the point in verse 6, just as we received Jesus by faith, the resulting walk of the Christian life is to be by faith. How do we receive Christ in our life? We didn't offer Him anything in exchange for salvation, the forgiveness of sins, or eternal life. No, these things were offered to us freely by His grace and received by faith. It wasn't our good works, holy living, fasting, and prayer, or church attendance, etc., that earned these things for us.

Unfortunately, after receiving Christ by faith in His grace, many fall back into a performance mentality thinking they earn God's blessing by works. That is not walking in the same way they received Christ! **If we started by faith in His grace, we should continue by faith in His grace.** Paul made this very point in Galatians 3:2–3,

This only I want to learn from you: Did you receive the Spirit by the works of the law, or by the hearing of faith? Are you so foolish? Having begun in the Spirit, are you now being made perfect by the flesh?

Verse 7 (quoted above) establishes for us a lifelong principle for our "walk in Him." Paul likens our journey to a tree. A tree starts as a seed planted in the ground. Much growth takes place before the tree is firmly established and can withstand the elements. Likewise, a Christian who is saved and stuck is in a vulnerable position! We are to be established in faith by being rooted and built up in Him! Just as a mature tree is able to stand strong in the storm, we will be able to stand strong if we are established in a mature faith. The more you use your faith by walking in it daily, the stronger and more mature you will become. The strong root system of your faith will provide stability in your life to endure storms! (Matthew 7:24–25).

Notice the last phrase, *"abounding in it with thanksgiving."* You need to know faith is never complete until there is thanksgiving. Your walk of faith must include thankfulness for all God has done and how He has blessed your life. Count your blessings, give thanks. Thankfulness will cause your faith to abound.

Father, I want to be rooted and built up in You and established in faith.

Amen!

DAY 27

The Law of Faith

Where is boasting then? It is excluded. By what law? Of works? No, but by the law of faith.

(Romans 3:27)

The Kingdom of God is governed by spiritual law. God's Kingdom is one of order, not anarchy and chaos. Please understand, when I use the term "law," I am not referring to the Old Testament Law of Moses. The Law of Moses was only given for a time until Christ came (Galatians 3:23–24). But that does not mean God's Kingdom is lawless. Notice the Apostle Paul used this exact terminology in today's verse, *"but by the **law** of faith."* The Kingdom of God is advanced on a principle of faith. As one lays hold of the will of God by faith, the kingdom is established in their life.

If we would begin to view faith as a law, we would get very different results. As an example, gravity is a law. The fact that there is a constant gravitational pull on earth makes it a law. It is not a variable. It is at work constantly, so we come to rely upon it at all times. We are able to walk, run, sit, or drive a car because of its constant effect. If it would suddenly spike or cease for a moment, it wouldn't be a law. Often people view faith as something which sometimes works and doesn't work at other times.

Because faith is a law, we can rely upon it. We know God requires it of us, so **we should expect it to work for us as our part in cooperating with God.** We should develop a confidence in the power of our faith which produces an assurance to receive from God. Often, people lack this assurance because of a misunderstanding about God. They have heard, *"For My thoughts are not your thoughts, nor are your ways My ways,' says the Lord"* (Isaiah 55:8) and develop the idea you can't ever tell about God. I want to tell you, this is the reason you have a Bible, so God's ways won't be mysterious to you!

We can take hold of His promises by the law of faith with an attitude that will not let go, expecting our faith to produce the result God has promised us! **The Kingdom of God is established in our lives as we embrace the will of God by the law of faith.** The promises God has made to us by His grace are received by employing the law of faith.

Father, I believe Your promises are mine by the law of faith. Amen!

DAY 28

Faith to be Made Well

And He said to her, "Daughter, your faith has made you well. Go in peace, and be healed of your affliction."

(Mark 5:34)

This is the incredible story of the healing of the woman with the issue of blood. We are told this woman had this affliction for twelve years! She had spent much on physicians but was not better; she had gotten worse (Mark 5:25–26). Her situation gave no hope for her, that is until she heard about Jesus! She then released her faith statement,

For she said, "If only I may touch His clothes, I shall be made well."

(Mark 5:28)

She broke Levitical Law (Leviticus 15:19–33) by pressing through the crowd to touch the hem of Jesus' garment. When she did, the Bible says, *"Immediately the fountain of her blood was dried up, and she felt in her body that she was healed of the affliction"* (vs. 29). Jesus sensed power had flowed out of Him and said,

"Who touched Me?" (vs. 31). He didn't even know she was there! This illustrates something very powerful for us. Healing is governed by spiritual law!

She was the only person in the crowd who received healing because she was the only one in the crowd who placed a demand on the anointing by the law of faith. This story disproves the idea this was a sovereign act of God to heal her. Probably everyone in the crowd had a need; thus, the reason they thronged Him. But she was the only one in the crowd drawing on His power by faith. This is exactly what Jesus told her in today's verse (quoted above).

This woman received her healing by applying the law of faith even before Jesus became aware of her presence! Someone may argue, "Jesus is God and knows all things!" Jesus was one hundred percent God in His spirit, but He was one hundred percent man in His flesh. He operated as a sinless man by receiving from His Father by faith and not according to divine privilege (Philippians 2:7). This illustrates for us **healing is governed by spiritual law and not a case-by-case decision from God based on His feelings for us!**

You will not receive the miracle, provision, or protection you need from God by begging Him. You will have to make a positive response to what He has done for you by exercising your faith to receive. God knows our needs, and He hears our cries, but our faith accesses His power and grace!

Father, I believe in the power of the law of faith to receive from You! Amen!

DAY 29

Thankfulness is an Expression of Faith

And one of them, when he saw that he was healed, returned,
and with a loud voice glorified God,

(Luke 17:15)

Thankfulness to the Lord for who He is and what He has done is a very important part of the Christian life, but it's easy to neglect when we are experiencing problems or challenges.

There is a wonderful story recorded in Luke 17:11–19. It says Jesus passed through Samaria and Galilee and came to a village where He met ten men who were lepers. From afar off, they lifted up their voices and said, *"Jesus, Master, have mercy on us!"* Verse 14 tells us Jesus said to them, *"Go, show yourselves to the priests."*

The men did as Jesus commanded them, and the verse says, *"And so it was as they went, they were cleansed."* These lepers weren't healed instantly; they were healed as they went. One of them, when he saw he was healed, returned and with a loud voice glorified God and gave Jesus thanks!

Relatively few people who receive the goodness of the Lord return to give Him thanks! But that doesn't prevent God from doing good. God doesn't do good things for us because we will do what is right. No, He does good because He is good, even if we don't do what is right! Jesus healed all ten according to their request, and nine of them didn't show proper appreciation.

Jesus told the one who returned to give thanks, "...*Arise, go thy way: thy faith hath made thee whole*" (vs. 19, KJV). **Ten were healed, but only one was made whole!** Giving thanks is a great expression of our faith—especially when we give thanks to God even before we see the results. Giving thanks to God means we take our eyes off of ourselves and our situation and focus on Him. It is a key that makes you "whole," not just "healed"!

Over and over in the Bible, we are encouraged to give thanks to God, to praise Him, and to acknowledge what He has done. You just can't over emphasize the importance of this! It's easy for us as believers to praise and thank Him when things are going well for us. Our flesh feels justified in griping and complaining when things aren't going so well. When you are tempted to be depressed or discouraged, take an inventory of your blessings. Then thank and praise your way to victory!

Father God, I'm sorry for the times I forget to say, "Thank you." Help me to keep my eyes on You and always to be thankful. I praise You and thank you today; things are as good as they are!
Amen!

DAY 30

Faith Believes the Word

Jesus said to him, 'Go your way; your son lives.' So the man believed the word that Jesus spoke to him, and he went his way.

(John 4:50)

Jesus had come to Cana of Galilee where a certain nobleman came to Him to ask Him to heal his son who was sick in Capernaum. The Bible says the boy was at the point of death, and the father wanted Jesus to go to Capernaum to heal him before he died. Verse 50 tells us,

...the man believed the word that Jesus spoke to him, and he went his way.

The story goes on to say his son was healed the day before at the very same hour Jesus spoke those words! There are some really important lessons to learn from this. Sometimes we think we know how things ought to be done and have certain expectations about them. The man thought Jesus had to be physically present to heal his son. Jesus wasn't even in the same city as the boy and spoke the word only for him to be healed!

But also notice it says, *"the man believed the word that Jesus spoke to him."* We have a part to play in receiving from God and establishing His will in our lives. Some believe it is all up to God, and whatever He wants done gets done. **But God is not working in your life independent of you; no, He works in you, through you.** You have to believe and cooperate by faith. This man brought the power of God into his crisis situation by cooperating with God by believing Jesus' words.

The way you view God's Word determines the way you will relate to God. The person who simply believes the written Word of God is operating in a much higher form of faith than the one who requires additional proof. As believers, we shouldn't require a sign as proof to believe. No, we believe because of the written Word. Some people challenge and assault the Bible, claiming it was written by men and therefore subject to error. It is true the Bible was written by men, but it was written by men who were inspired by the Holy Spirit (2 Peter 1:21; 2 Timothy 3:16–17). Often, I tell people, "It matters what you believe." When you experience challenges in life, or even when things are going well, you need to know it really does matter that we believe the right things.

Father God, I am a believer, not a doubter. I believe Your Word is alive and powerful, and I receive it by faith!

In Jesus' name, I pray...

Amen!

DAY 31

Your Most Holy Faith

But you, beloved, building yourselves up on your most holy faith, praying in the Holy Spirit.

(Jude 1:20)

We understand, and I have made the point that "*...faith comes by hearing, and hearing by the word of God*" from Romans 10:17. It is most important for us to hear and receive the Word of God to build faith within us. **The Word of God is faith's point of origin.** But this verse brings out another dynamic that is important to understand. We build ourselves up on our "*most holy faith, praying in the Holy Spirit.*" This is a reference to praying in other tongues.

If you have received the baptism with the Holy Spirit and have been given the supernatural ability to speak/pray in other tongues (Acts 2:4, 10:45–46, 19:6), I encourage you to do it often! As you do, know that you are building yourself up on your most holy faith! This is a way God has provided for us to be built up in Him. 1 Corinthians 14:4 says, "*He who speaks in a tongue edifies himself...*" The word "edifies" means to "build up" as if charging yourself like you would charge a battery! If you have not received the gift of the baptism with the Holy Spirit and speaking with other tongues, I encourage you to seek God to receive this supernatural equipping!

The Holy Spirit is a tremendous help in our prayer lives. Let's look at Romans 8:26, *"Likewise the Spirit also helps in our weaknesses. For we do not know what we should pray for as we ought, but the Spirit Himself makes intercession for us with groanings which cannot be uttered."* This has been an encouraging scripture for countless believers. Certainly, none of us know exactly how to pray in every situation. It is a great comfort to know the Holy Spirit is there to help us. When, in the natural, you have exhausted your knowledge of the problem and no longer know what to pray, allow the Holy Spirit to lead you and intercede through you.

In this way, you are able to bypass the difficulties posed by your limited knowledge in the natural and begin to tap into His unlimited knowledge and allow Him to lead you and help you to pray the perfect will of God! (see Romans 8:27). Understanding this will cause you to be built up immensely on your most holy faith, and your confidence will soar.

Heavenly Father, I thank you for the presence of the Holy Spirit within me to help me and build me up on my most holy faith!

Amen!

(For more information on the baptism with the Holy Spirit, see devotions on days 38–41.)

DAY 32

Mix Faith with the Gospel

For indeed the gospel was preached to us as well as to them;
but the word which they heard did not profit them, not being
mixed with faith in those who heard it.

(Hebrews 4:2)

The Gospel is the power of God according to Romans 1:16, *"For I am not ashamed of the gospel of Christ, for it is the power of God to salvation for everyone who believes, for the Jew first and also for the Greek."* So, why is it some people benefit greatly from hearing the Gospel preached and not others? The answer is in today's verse (Hebrews 4:2), **the Gospel must be mixed with faith in those who hear it!**

Be assured, the Gospel and the Word of God are powerful. Jeremiah 1:12 says, *"Then the Lord said to me, 'You have seen well, for I am ready to perform My word.'"* God is faithful to watch over His Word to perform it, but we have to partner with Him by placing faith in what He has said! Romans 3:3–4 addresses this issue,

For what if some did not believe? Will their unbelief make the faithfulness of God without effect? Certainly not! Indeed, let God be true but every man a liar...

The phrase in verse 4, *"let God be true but every man a liar,"* is the response to the question in verse 3. Paul is saying God and His promises are always true even if men don't believe them. We must always acknowledge the integrity of God and His Word. Man's belief or unbelief does not negate God and His Word.

A person can make God's Word of no effect in their life, but God's Word doesn't lose any power. Mark 7:13 says, *"Making the word of God of no effect through your tradition which you have handed down. And many such things you do."* Our disbelief, tradition, or doubt will hinder the effectiveness of God's Word in our lives. Many who do not recognize this falsely conclude God or His Word have failed them when they should recognize, God isn't the problem.

It is important to recognize our responsibility to mix faith with the Gospel in order to establish God's will in our lives.

The time is fulfilled, and the kingdom of God is at hand. Repent, and believe in the gospel.

(Mark 1:15)

Father, I believe in Your integrity. I join my faith together with what You have done to receive provision in my life. Thank you for it.
In Jesus' name, I pray...
Amen!

DAY 33

Full of Faith and Power

*And Stephen, full of faith and power, did great wonders and
signs among the people.*

(Acts 6:8)

The Bible records Jesus' response to various degrees of faith
operating in people's lives. He marveled at the Roman Centurion's "great faith" (Matthew 8:10). He said to His own disciples,
"Why are you so fearful? How is it that you have no faith?" (Mark
4:40). Clearly, it is possible for people to operate at various lev-
els of faith in their personal lives.

Today's verse tells us Stephen *"full of faith and power, did great
wonders and signs among the people."* Stephen was not named an
apostle, nor any of the other five-fold ministry gifts (Ephesians
4:11), but he was used by God to perform great signs and wonders. Sometimes people have the idea only gifted ministers or
special people can be used by God in the supernatural. Some
seem to think you have to be a "super-duper" to see the supernatural power of God flow through you or work on your behalf.
This story about Stephen de-bunks that theory! **This proves
believers can be full of faith and can be used to operate in the
supernatural power of God in their lives.**

Stephen was chosen by the congregation to serve among the first group of deacons in the early church (Acts 6:5). He was apparently a good man who met the qualifications prescribed, *"...seek out from among you seven men of good reputation, full of the Holy Spirit and wisdom, whom we may appoint over this business"* (Acts 6:3). His role was to serve the church by ministering to the needs of the congregation.

As he began to be used by God performing "great wonders and signs among the people," he was falsely accused by certain sects of the Jews and placed on trial. His defense, which was a powerful discourse of Jewish history, is recorded in Chapter 7. When his accusers came under conviction and could stand it no longer, they stoned him to death. As the first martyr of the church was dying, Acts 7:56 records these amazing words, *"...Look! I see the heavens opened and the Son of Man standing at the right hand of God!"* This is the only occurrence in all of Scripture recording Jesus standing at the Father's right hand! It would seem Jesus was honoring Stephen's faith as his life was being taken from him! This serves as another example of Jesus' respect for the faith of His people!

Father, I desire to be full of faith to be able to be used by You!
In Jesus' name...
Amen!

Part Two:

THE HOLY SPIRIT
God's Gift to the Church

Introduction

I have chosen to title this section The Holy Spirit: God's Gift to the Church because of Jesus' statement in John 14:17,

> *the Spirit of truth, whom the world cannot receive, because it neither sees Him nor knows Him; but you know Him, for He dwells with you and will be in you.*

The Holy Spirit is indeed a great gift given to us by our good God! You will find I have dedicated each daily devotion to various workings of the Spirit in the lives of Christians. It is amazing how many times the Holy Spirit is spoken of in Scripture. He is also referred to in various ways, such as the Spirit of God, the Spirit of the Lord, the Spirit of the Living God, the Spirit of Christ, the Spirit of grace, and others.

There are far too many references to cover them all in this short work, but I have attempted to unpack as much as possible in this devotional, and my hope is you will gain a deeper understanding and appreciation for the presence, power, and working of the Holy Spirit in your life!

If you will make an effort to look up the scriptures in your Bible, pray, and meditate on each one using this devotional as a study guide, I believe the Lord will reveal Himself to you, and you will grow in your knowledge of the Spirit of God. May our good God bless you as you read!

—Chaplain McComb

DAY 34

The Spirit of the Lord Brings Freedom

Now the Lord is the Spirit; and where the Spirit of the Lord is, there is liberty.

(2 Corinthians 3:17)

One of the greatest revelations we receive concerning our new life in Christ is, *"He has delivered us from the power of darkness and conveyed us into the kingdom of the Son of His love, in whom we have redemption through His blood, the forgiveness of sins"* (Colossians 1:13–14). We are no longer under the dominion of the power of darkness. We have been taken out of the devil's kingdom and placed into God's Kingdom as His children when we are born again!

The Apostle Paul describes what we receive as children of God in today's verse, *"where the Spirit of the Lord is, there is **liberty**."* Praise the Lord; this is great news for us! This liberty is freedom from the law of sin and death (Romans 8:2), freedom from the bondage of the devil (1 John 3:8), and even religious bondage in any form that would bind us as believers.

Who gave Himself for our sins, that He might deliver us from this present evil age, according to the will of our God and Father.

(Galatians 1:4)

The Spirit of the Lord brings us freedom in Christ, and we are instructed by the Apostle Paul to *"Stand fast therefore in the liberty by which Christ has made us free, and do not be entangled again with a yoke of bondage"* (Galatians 5:1). Prior to our conversion to Christ, we were under the influence of all kinds of slavery from evil spirits, torment, and fear, as well as other types of oppression from the devil. In contrast to that, there is now freedom and an exemption from bondage and care available to those who will receive it by faith! In addition to these spiritual bondages, there is a freedom from religious bondage to the law seen in Romans 7:6,

But now we have been delivered from the law, having died to what we were held by, so that we should serve in the newness of the Spirit and not in the oldness of the letter.

The Law of the Spirit of life in Christ Jesus has made us free from the Law of sin and death! (Romans 8:2). The Spirit of the Lord has enabled us to live free from the bondage of the devil and religious law so we can stand fast in the liberty Christ has given to make us free!

Father, I thank you that Your Spirit has given me liberty and freedom. I will stand fast in this freedom from You!
Amen!

DAY 35

Jesus Needed the Holy Spirit

When He had been baptized, Jesus came up immediately from the water; and behold, the heavens were opened to Him, and He saw the Spirit of God descending like a dove and alighting upon Him. And suddenly a voice came from heaven, saying, "This is My beloved Son, in whom I am well pleased."

(Matthew 3:16–17)

This shows us the necessity of the presence of the Holy Spirit in the life of man. Jesus would need all of God's power present with Him to accomplish all God sent Him to do. Philippians 2:5–7 tells us, *"Let this mind be in you which was also in Christ Jesus, who, being in the form of God, did not consider it robbery to be equal with God, but made Himself of no reputation, taking the form of a bondservant, and coming in the likeness of men."* Jesus stripped Himself of all divine privilege when He humbled Himself to become a man. Jesus was one hundred percent God **and** one hundred percent man. He was sinless man, but He became a man to fulfill God's redemptive plan for mankind.

As a Man (stripped of divine privilege), He ministered according to all the laws of the Kingdom of God and needed the anointing of the Holy Spirit to operate in the power of God. If Jesus needed the Holy Spirit with Him in His life, how much more do we need the Holy Spirit in our life? Jesus didn't even begin His earthly ministry before receiving the anointing of the Holy Spirit. Everything Jesus did, His preaching, performing miracles, healing the sick, raising the dead, casting out demons, even His victory over sin—He did by the power of the Holy Spirit! (Matthew 12:28).

If Jesus Himself could do nothing without the power of the Holy Spirit, how much more do we need the empowering presence of the Holy Spirit in our life? Living the Christian life in our own strength is not just hard to do; it is impossible in our own natural abilities. The almighty power of God manifests through human beings by the power of the Spirit. It is a great privilege and honor given to us to have the presence of God's Spirit resident in us to help us in life's journey! As Christians, we belong to God and should have the desire to serve and please Him. The Holy Spirit is with us to empower and help us to do it!

Father God, I thank you for the precious Holy Spirit's presence with me. Teach me to submit to His leadership daily!
Amen!

DAY 36

Jesus Was Led by the Holy Spirit

Then Jesus was led up by the Spirit into the wilderness to be tempted by the devil.

(Matthew 4:1)

After Jesus' water baptism by John the Baptist and God's audible voice declaring His love and pleasure with Jesus, the Holy Spirit led Jesus into the wilderness for the purpose of being tempted by the devil. However, Jesus taught His disciples to pray, in what we refer to as the Lord's Prayer, that they would not be led into temptation (Matthew 6:13). There are things Jesus suffered for us that we should not suffer.

God has made it clear for us He does not tempt us, *"Let no one say when he is tempted, 'I am tempted by God'; for God cannot be tempted by evil, nor does He Himself tempt anyone"* (James 1:13). In this case, Jesus was led by the Spirit to be tempted and overcome the temptation so we would not be led into temptation. Jesus did not fall for any of the devil's temptations or tricks. He was able to overcome every one of them by quoting the written Word of God! There is a great lesson for us in this.

We should never think when we are facing temptation, God is using it or testing us. God does not use temptation this way. Temptation can originate from the devil or our fleshly desires, but both can be resisted and overcome the same way Jesus overcame by quoting the inspired Word of God! The devil brought three specific temptations to Jesus, and each time Jesus resisted the temptation by quoting from the Book of Deuteronomy. This means the Scripture was valuable enough to Him to memorize large portions of it. When Jesus needed it, He simply drew from the reservoir of Scripture He had committed to memory and used it as a two-edged sword (Hebrews 4:12) to war in the spirit realm.

> *No temptation has overtaken you except what is common to mankind. And God is faithful; he will not let you be tempted beyond what you can bear. But when you are tempted, he will also provide a way out so that you can endure it.*
>
> (1 Corinthians 10:13 NIV)

You can rely upon the Holy Spirit within you to help you to overcome. The Holy Spirit will lead you by bringing Scripture to mind to use to bring victory! (John 14:26). **We should be putting Scripture in our hearts daily so the Holy Spirit can help us access it!**

Father, I want to hide Your Word in my heart and be led by Your Spirit to help me.
Amen!

DAY 37

Jesus Returned in the Power of the Spirit

Then Jesus returned in the power of the Spirit to Galilee, and news of Him went out through all the surrounding region.

(Luke 4:14)

When the devil had ended every temptation in the wilderness, he departed from Jesus, and we are told in today's verse, *"Jesus returned in the power of the Spirit"* and then began His Galilean ministry. After having received the Holy Spirit, Jesus was now ready to begin His ministry. The effectiveness of His ministry depended upon the empowering presence of the Holy Spirit in Him. Notice it says the *"news of Him went out through all the surrounding region."* His Galilean ministry has been referred to as the year of His popularity. Jesus began to operate in the power of the Spirit, performing signs, wonders, and miracles, the news of which began to spread far and wide as He became known.

Just as Jesus relied upon the empowering presence of the Holy Spirit in His life, we should rely upon the Holy Spirit's presence in ours as well. We make a poor imitation of Christ and representative of Him in our own strength and abilities. After having received the Holy Spirit in our lives, people should notice a difference in us. Indeed, there is a difference in us as Christians. People should notice more victory in our lives than the unbeliever who lives next door. We should display peace, joy, and power over temptation unknown to those who are not in relationship with God. There is an enabling power available to every Christian known as the baptism with the Holy Spirit, which I will begin to describe in the following pages of this devotional.

Getting saved is not the end of our journey with the Lord; it is merely the beginning. Too many Christians are saved and stuck. Don't stay at the cross; go on to Pentecost and receive the empowering presence of the Holy Spirit, which will enable you to operate in the power of the Spirit as well. Jesus commanded this of His disciples prior to His departure in Luke 24:49, *"Behold, I send the Promise of My Father upon you; but tarry in the city of Jerusalem until you are endued with power from on high."* As important as the Great Commission (Matthew 28:18–20) was, and is, Jesus didn't even want them to begin without receiving the Promise of the Father, which is the baptism with the Holy Spirit providing the Spiritual empowerment they would need to be effective. And so do you.

Father, I am thankful You have made the power of the Spirit available to me.

Amen!

DAY 38

The Holy Spirit Promised

And being assembled together with them, He commanded them not to depart from Jerusalem, but to wait for the Promise of the Father, "which," He said, "you have heard from Me; for John truly baptized with water, but you shall be baptized with the Holy Spirit not many days from now."

(Acts 1:4–5)

The Book of Acts was written by Luke, who also authored the third gospel, which bears his name. You could think of Acts as Luke 2. He actually picks up right where he left off in Luke, Chapter 24, with his reference in today's verse to *"wait for the Promise of the Father."* Verse 5 (quoted above) tells us what the **"Promise of the Father" is —the baptism with the Holy Spirit.**

Immediately before He ascended to heaven, Jesus gave the disciples one final command, *"Behold, I send the Promise of My Father upon you; but tarry in the city of Jerusalem until you are endued with power from on high"* (Luke 24:49). Jesus had previously told His disciples it would be in their best interest if He went away because He would send the Holy Spirit to them (John 16:7). Today's verse 5 confirms that promise.

Acts 1:8 further confirms His promise to them, *"But you shall receive power when the Holy Spirit has come upon you; and you shall be witnesses to Me in Jerusalem, and in all Judea and Samaria, and to the end of the earth"* (Acts 1:8), which is exactly what happened on the Day of Pentecost (Acts 2:1–4). Acts 1:8 reveals the purpose of the baptism with the Holy Spirit. The purpose is not speaking in tongues; although you get to speak in tongues as part of it, the purpose of the baptism with the Holy Spirit is the power to be a witness and power for life and service!

In the days of the early Church, it was the norm for believers to receive the baptism with the Holy Spirit. I'm sad to say it is far from being the norm nowadays, but not because God is less willing to give the Holy Spirit to believers now than He was then. It is because many believers today are unwilling to receive the Promise of the Father. Unfortunately, among the worldwide Church, many believers and even whole denominations have rejected their own means of empowerment! I encourage you to educate yourself about this and be willing to receive this most important gift from God!

Father, I'm thankful You have made it possible to receive the precious Holy Spirit as Your gift to the Church!
Amen!

DAY 39

The Outpouring of the Holy Spirit

And they were all filled with the Holy Spirit and began to speak with other tongues, as the Spirit gave them utterance.

(Acts 2:4)

Acts, Chapter 2, speaks of the Jewish holiday of Pentecost where we find Jesus' disciples doing just as He commanded them before His ascension to heaven. There were one hundred twenty of them (Acts 1:15) gathered together in an upper room, all in one accord, when *"...suddenly there came a sound from heaven, as of a rushing mighty wind, and it filled the whole house where they were sitting"* (Acts 2:2). This verse is describing the initial outpouring of the Holy Spirit in the history of the world! These were the first believers to ever receive the baptism with the Holy Spirit, which was promised by Jesus (Acts 1:4).

The Holy Spirit came into the room as a sound of a rushing, mighty wind. It wasn't a wind; it was the sound of a rushing wind along with a manifestation of the glory of God, which looked like the room was on fire (Acts 2:3). One hundred twenty disciples of the Lord *"...were all filled with the Holy Spirit and began to speak with other tongues, as the Spirit gave them utterance"* (Acts

2:4). These believers were the first to receive the mighty baptism with the Holy Spirit as promised by Jesus! It is interesting John the Baptist announced it would happen this way,

> *I indeed baptize you with water unto repentance, but He who is coming after me is mightier than I, whose sandals I am not worthy to carry. He will baptize you with the Holy Spirit and fire.*
>
> (Matthew 3:11)

This event, which radically changed the lives of Jesus' followers, was accompanied by a great manifestation! In that instant, an amazing transformation took place in those believers. Peter is a great example of a life that was changed. On three occasions, he denied even knowing Jesus (John 18:17, 25, and 27), but on that day, he stood up and began to preach an impromptu sermon, and three thousand people were saved! Something had changed Peter from a fearful fisherman to a powerful preacher! There can only be one explanation for this; it was this experience of receiving the baptism with the Holy Spirit. The baptism with the Holy Spirit is an endowment of power upon us, which enables us to be a witness and empowers us for life and service. You can receive this now if you are a believer and are ready to receive Him by faith.

Father, I want to receive this empowering baptism with the Holy Spirit!

Amen!

(Turn to the appendix of this devotional for a prayer to receive the baptism with the Holy Spirit).

DAY 40

You Shall Receive the Gift of the Holy Spirit

Then Peter said to them, "Repent, and let every one of you
be baptized in the name of Jesus Christ for the remission of
sins; and you shall receive the gift of the Holy Spirit."

(Acts 2:38)

After having received the baptism with the Holy Spirit, Peter stands up on the Day of Pentecost and preaches his first sermon! The transforming power of the Holy Spirit within Peter was evident as he was emboldened to take the leadership role and preach an impromptu sermon resulting in about three thousand people being saved! (Acts 2:41).

An international gathering of Jews was present, having gathered together at Jerusalem to celebrate the festival of Pentecost. When they all heard the sounds of the rushing, mighty wind and the speaking in tongues, "*...they were all amazed and perplexed, saying to one another, 'Whatever could this mean?' Others mocking said, 'They are full of new wine'*" (Acts 2:12–13). Peter stood up and began to explain it as a fulfillment of prophecy spoken by the prophet Joel (vs. 16).

Emboldened by the power of the Spirit, he preached Jesus as the Christ stating, *"Him, being delivered by the determined purpose and foreknowledge of God, you have taken by lawless hands, have crucified, and put to death; whom God raised up, having loosed the pains of death, because it was not possible that He should be held by it"* (Acts 2:23–24). This is evidence he had been transformed from a fearful fisherman to a powerful preacher! He ended his sermon with verse 38 (quoted above). Can you see the mercy of our good God in that statement? The ones who called for Jesus' death were now told even they could receive the Holy Spirit baptism!

Acts 2:39 states, *"For the promise is to you and to your children, and to all who are afar off, as many as the Lord our God will call."* What promise? The Promise of the Father (Acts 1:4–5) was for them and all who are afar off! This is for us as well, still available, still relevant! It hasn't passed away; it was not just for the early Church. **This should be the normal experience for every Christian!** This theologically proves the experience is valid for us today! It is available to you to be received by faith! As this truth is being presented to you, it is causing faith to come alive within you to receive it. You simply need to make the decision to receive the Promise!

Father, thank you for making the Promise of the Father available to me! I want to be empowered by Your Spirit as well!
Amen!

DAY 41

We Must Receive the Holy Spirit

Now when the apostles who were at Jerusalem heard that Samaria had received the word of God, they sent Peter and John to them, who, when they had come down, prayed for them that they might receive the Holy Spirit.

(Acts 8:14–15)

An important example of believers receiving the Holy Spirit is recorded in Acts, Chapter 8. As a result of the persecution of the Church led by Saul of Tarsus, there was a scattering of the believers who went everywhere preaching the Word (Acts 8:4). Phillip went to Samaria and sparked a great revival! (Acts 8:5–8). As Phillip preached Christ to the Samaritans, multitudes of people received signs, wonders, and miracles, and there was "... *great joy in that city"* (vs. 8).

When the news spread to the leaders of the church at Jerusalem, they sent Peter and John to help with the revival (see today's verse quoted above). We're told, when they arrived, they prayed for the people to receive the Holy Spirit. Acts 8:16–17 tells us, *"For as yet He had fallen upon none of them. They had only been baptized in the name of the Lord Jesus. Then they laid hands on them, and they received the Holy Spirit."* This is one of the clearest examples in the Bible showing the New Birth and the Holy Spirit baptism are separate experiences! We are told they had already been water baptized. We know Phillip would not have baptized them in water unless they were born again!

Peter and John laid hands on them, and they were then filled with the Holy Spirit, clearly illustrating that the baptism with the Holy Spirit is distinct from and subsequent to the new birth. This shows us clearly the early Church considered Holy Spirit baptism to be the very next experience to be received from the Lord. It was normal Christianity which was available to all believers to be received. Notice it says they *"prayed for them that they might receive the Holy Spirit."* **The baptism with the Holy Spirit is a free gift offered to believers, but it must be received by faith!** Peter and John had a part to play in this, but so did the believers. Believers must receive the gift by faith. The experience doesn't just happen to you as a sovereign act of God. No, you must cooperate with God to receive this gift by faith!

If you are ready to receive the Holy Spirit, turn to the appendix in the back of this book for a prayer to receive the Holy Spirit baptism!

Father God, I will receive Your Spirit today! Amen!

DAY 42

Gentiles Received the Holy Spirit

And those of the circumcision who believed were astonished, as many as came with Peter, because the gift of the Holy Spirit had been poured out on the Gentiles also. For they heard them speak with tongues and magnify God.

(Acts 10:45–46)

Acts, Chapter 10, contains a very important reference to the infilling of the Holy Spirit for us to consider. This is when the Gentiles first received the Promise of the Father. In the opening verses of Chapter 10, we are introduced to a Roman Centurion by the name of Cornelius. While he was in prayer seeking God, he saw in a vision an angel of God (vs.3) with a message from God for him, *"Your prayers and your alms have come up for a memorial before God. Now send men to Joppa, and send for Simon whose surname is Peter"* (vs. 4–5).

Cornelius did as the Lord commanded him; when the men found Peter, they asked him to return with them to meet Cornelius. After arriving back at Cornelius' house, they found that in anticipation of Peter's arrival, Cornelius had gathered together a crowd of family and friends. After their introduction to one another, Peter began to preach to the group. In the sermon, Peter gave a brief but descriptive summary of the life and ministry of Jesus, and *"while Peter was still speaking these words, the Holy Spirit fell upon all those who heard the word"* (v. 44). It happened just as it had happened on the Day of Pentecost—Peter had not stopped to lay hands on them, and yet they were all filled with the Holy Spirit!

Verse 46 clearly says, *"For they heard them speak with tongues and magnify God."* Peter and the Jewish Christians present with him knew the Gentiles had received because they heard them speaking in other tongues. This makes it clear to us, speaking in tongues is at least one initial evidence of being filled with the Holy Spirit. Because of this, the Jewish leadership now knew for a certainty God was not only dealing with Jews! (Acts 11:15–18). **This is one of the most important events recorded in the Book of Acts because it shows Gentiles converted to Christianity and being filled with the Holy Spirit!** Can I get a great amen from all the Gentiles, please?! Just as this experience proved to the Jewish leadership God's dealings with Gentiles, it likewise proves it theologically to us as well!

Father, I'm thankful You have made this experience available to all! Amen!

DAY 43

Did You Receive the Holy Spirit When You Believed?

He said to them, "Did you receive the Holy Spirit when you believed?" So they said to him, "We have not so much as heard whether there is a Holy Spirit."

(Acts 19:2)

Paul's third missionary journey brought his return to Ephesus. We are told he found disciples when he arrived there (vs. 2). A minister by the name of Apollos had already been there. Apollos was an eloquent man and mighty in the Scriptures (Acts 18:24) who had apparently received his revelation of the Messiah from John the Baptist but somehow missed the Day of Pentecost and was unaware of the outpouring of the Holy Spirit. Apollos had been preaching Jesus as the Christ and baptizing with a baptism of repentance, according to John's way (Acts 19:3–4).

When Paul arrived at Ephesus and learned of these disciples, he discovered their experience was incomplete! They had *"not so much as heard whether there is a Holy Spirit"* (vs. 2). His next question to them was, "'*Into what then were you baptized?*' *So they said, 'Into John's baptism'*" (vs. 3). These men were genuinely born again by believing on Jesus, who had come to die for their sins, but they had not been baptized with the Holy Spirit. Paul was not okay with it! Paul then explained to them,

> ... "*John indeed baptized with a baptism of repentance, saying to the people that they should believe on Him who would come after him, that is, on Christ Jesus.*" *When they heard this, they were baptized in the name of the Lord Jesus.*
>
> (Acts 19:4–5)

This proves to us scripturally that the baptism with the Holy Spirit was part of the gospel Paul preached! Often, I find believers in this same spiritual state. They are born again but have not received the Promise of the Father. **This should be the next experience for those who have received Jesus.** After having corrected their spiritual condition, Acts 19:6 says, "*And when Paul had laid hands on them, the Holy Spirit came upon them, and they spoke with tongues and prophesied.*" Once these men were born again, there was no need for them to wait to be filled with the Holy Spirit. This should solidify for us that this is the New Testament pattern! If you have not yet received the Holy Spirit, this is the next experience for you as well!

Father, I praise You for Your gift of the Holy Spirit to the Church! I believe the promise of the Spirit is for me!
Amen!

DAY 44

God's Gift to the Church

*The Spirit of truth, whom the world cannot receive, because
it neither sees Him nor knows Him; but you know Him, for
He dwells with you and will be in you.*

(John 14:17)

Jesus makes a very important statement in today's verse
that must be understood. The term *"The Spirit of Truth"* is a reference to the Holy Spirit. Jesus clearly said the world cannot
receive the Holy Spirit! This means a person who is not born
again cannot receive the Holy Spirit. Jesus is God's gift to the
world, according to John 3:16, *"For God so loved the world that He
gave His only begotten Son, that whoever believes in Him should not
perish but have everlasting life."* The Holy Spirit is God's gift to the
Church! This needs some explanation.

Humans must receive the quickening of the Holy Spirit to
discern spiritual things. This is what Paul said in 1 Corinthians 2:14, *"But the natural man does not receive the things of the Spirit
of God, for they are foolishness to him; nor can he know them, because
they are spiritually discerned."* This is why an unsaved, unregener-
ate man is unable to receive the Holy Spirit; he/she lacks spiritual discernment.

In today's verse, Jesus was speaking to His disciples. He made a clear distinction between the Holy Spirit being **with** them versus the Holy Spirit being **in** them. The Holy Spirit is always involved in all of God's dealings with man. This is evidenced by the fact that the disciples were able to know who Jesus was because the Holy Spirit was with them, revealing it to them, but Jesus clearly pointed out the Holy Spirit would be in them.

Some may argue that they have the Holy Spirit because no man can come to Jesus except through the ministry of the Holy Spirit. This thinking is based upon John 6:44, *"No one can come to Me unless the Father who sent Me draws him; and I will raise him up at the last day."* But remember, there is a difference between the Holy Spirit being **with** a person and Him being **in** a person. It is through the baptism with the Holy Spirit that He comes to live within the heart of the believer. Each of us as born-again Christians must make the decision to receive the baptism with the Holy Spirit in our lives, enabling the Holy Spirit to take up residence in our heart and empower us.

Heavenly Father, I'm thankful for the gift of the Holy Spirit to the Church!
Amen!

DAY 45

The Holy Spirit is Given to Those Who Ask

If a son asks for bread from any father among you, will he give him a stone? Or if he asks for a fish, will he give him a serpent instead of a fish? Or if he asks for an egg, will he offer him a scorpion? If you then, being evil, know how to give good gifts to your children, how much more will your heavenly Father give the Holy Spirit to those who ask Him!

(Luke 11:11–13)

In Luke, Chapter 11, Jesus is teaching on prayer, ministering assurance to us our Father is ready and willing to answer our prayers. He said, *"So I say to you, ask, and it will be given to you; seek, and you will find; knock, and it will be opened to you. For everyone who asks receives, and he who seeks finds, and to him who knocks it will be opened"* (Luke 11:9–10). We should be able to trust completely that our heavenly Father will grant our requests!

Jesus then illustrates this by showing how earthly fathers desire to answer their children's requests. Every good father wants to bless his children by giving them good gifts. Jesus makes the point that if human fathers know how to give good gifts to their children, *"how much more will your heavenly Father give the Holy Spirit to those who ask Him"* (vs.13). The most loving father in the world cannot compare with the love our heavenly Father has for us. And yet, often people doubt God's willingness to bless us.

I have made the point the Holy Spirit is God's gift to the Church. He is offered freely to all of God's people, but we do have to ask to receive Him into our lives. This is talking about the Promise of the Father, which is, the baptism with the Holy Spirit. Jesus making this statement, in the context of God's willingness to answer our prayers, should cause us to be confident when we ask for the Holy Spirit, we will not receive a counterfeit. When we ask for the Holy Spirit, we will not receive a serpent or a stone!

God is willing to give the Holy Spirit to any of His children who will ask for Him, but we must know it is our responsibility to receive the gift by faith. **You can be confident today God will give the Holy Spirit when you ask!**

Father, I believe the Holy Spirit is given to believers when we ask You for Him!

Amen!

DAY 46

Jesus Was Anointed with the Holy Spirit

How God anointed Jesus of Nazareth with the Holy Spirit and with power, who went about doing good and healing all who were oppressed by the devil, for God was with Him.

(Acts 10:38)

This verse was spoken by Peter as he was preaching to Cornelius' relatives and close friends and gives us a very descriptive summary of the ministry of Jesus. God anointed Jesus with the Holy Spirit and power! Notice it says Jesus used this anointing and power to do good and heal, not to do evil. This is one of God's main attributes and one of the clearest ways we have to discern what is from God and what is from the devil. God is good and does good (Psalm 119:68), and if something is bad, it is from the devil! (John 10:10). I have a simple theology concerning these things: **good God, bad devil.**

This verse teaches us those who needed healing were *"oppressed by the devil,"* which clearly shows sickness and disease are from the devil, not God. God would not have anointed His Son to undo something He was trying to accomplish! This seems clear to me; you would need to have someone help you to misunderstand this. However, we have had a lot of help to misunderstand God through bad teaching and wrong doctrine. Let's be sure to base our belief system on what the Bible says.

In Jesus' hometown synagogue in Nazareth, He stood up to read from the Book of the prophet Isaiah. *"...He found the place where it was written: 'The Spirit of the Lord is upon Me, because He has anointed Me to preach the gospel to the poor; He has sent Me to heal the brokenhearted, to proclaim liberty to the captives and recovery of sight to the blind, to set at liberty those who are oppressed'"* (Luke 4:17–18). This is an Old Testament passage about the coming Messiah, and Jesus applied it to Himself,

> *And He began to say to them, "Today this Scripture is ful-filled in your hearing."*
>
> (vs. 21)

Jesus undoubtedly understood this anointing He received from God was for the purpose of fulfilling Scripture and communicating a message from God to all mankind! Jesus was the express image of God (Hebrews 1:3) and represented God perfectly and manifested God's will for us. Jesus used the anointing to preach, heal, and proclaim liberty to captives and the oppressed so we can all be free!

Father, thank you for anointing Jesus to do good for all!
Amen!

DAY 47

The Holy Spirit Speaks

As they ministered to the Lord and fasted, the Holy Spirit said, "Now separate to Me Barnabas and Saul for the work to which I have called them."

(Acts 13:2)

This ministry took place at a church which had been established in a place called Antioch, Syria. The gospel had spread to the north of Israel, where a church had been established with new Gentile believers. Acts 11:22 tells us, *"Then news of these things came to the ears of the church in Jerusalem, and they sent out Barnabas to go as far as Antioch."* When the Jewish leadership heard about this church in Antioch, they sent a man named Barnabas to check it out. Barnabas was so pleased and excited at what he found in Antioch, he *"...encouraged them all that with purpose of heart they should continue with the Lord"* (Acts 11:23). Barnabas wanted to help establish this young church, so he went to Tarsus to seek Saul (Paul) and brought him back to Antioch, where they taught for a year (Acts 11:25–26). The Church became so grounded in Paul's doctrine of grace *"the disciples were first called Christians in Antioch."*

As the Church matured, leadership began to be established. Today's verse reveals an interesting thing for us. As the believers were ministering to the Lord while seeking Him through fasting and prayer, **the Holy Spirit spoke to them!** How did the Holy Spirit speak to these men? There is no indication it was an audible voice. It was likely a manifestation of the gifts of the Spirit, either prophecy, a word of knowledge, or a word of wisdom (1 Corinthians 12:8–10). The Holy Spirit communicated direction to the Church, which confirmed the call of God on those men's lives!

As a Christian, we can expect the Holy Spirit to speak direction to our lives as well! It can come through a seasoned leader in our life or through one of the gifts of the Spirit, but primarily God will speak to you from the Bible or the still small voice of His Spirit. God is a Spirit, and the main way He speaks to us is Spirit to spirit. You must learn to listen and discern His voice and leading coming from within your spirit. God loves you and wants to communicate direction for your life. As you minister to Him and draw near to Him, you become familiar with His leading. Begin to listen to the Spirit of God dealing with your spirit.

Father, I believe You can and do speak. I pray I will be sensitive to Your voice today!
Amen!

DAY 48

The Holy Spirit Directs Us

After they had come to Mysia, they tried to go into Bithynia, but the Spirit did not permit them.

(Acts 16:7)

Paul and Silas were ministering in a province of Asia Minor called Galatia on Paul's second missionary journey. Paul had previously ministered to the Galatians on his first missionary journey. He apparently desired to go into Bithynia (modern-day Turkey) to preach the gospel there, but the Holy Spirit forbade them. There is no explanation given as to why the Holy Spirit did not allow them to proceed in that direction. The Lord then ministered direction to Paul through a vision, *"And a vision appeared to Paul in the night. A man of Macedonia stood and pleaded with him, saying, 'Come over to Macedonia and help us'"* (Acts 16:9). This is what is commonly referred to as the Macedonian Call. Judging from the content of the vision, we can assume the people of Macedonia were hungry for the gospel.

Some people have the mistaken idea that we should not do anything without specific direction from the Lord. That is not the way Paul was operating. Paul was just going anywhere he desired to minister the gospel without relying upon God to give him specific instructions about where he was to go. They were going everywhere (Matthew 28:18–20) at their own discretion. Otherwise, the Holy Spirit would have contradicted Himself through the vision. Paul was not insensitive to the direction of the Spirit; when He received the vision, he followed it willingly!

This is a great lesson for us as believers today. We should listen to the Spirit of God for direction, but we do not have to wait for specific direction before we "go into all the world" (Mark 16:15). When ministering to others, we should not assume we have a red light. **We should assume we have a green light because the Bible tells us to go.** When it comes to making decisions that are not so clearly spelled out for us in the Word, we should rely upon the Holy Spirit as our guide. Psalm 32:8 says to us, *"I will instruct you and teach you in the way you should go; I will guide you with My eye."* We should certainly be open to receive instruction from the Lord as He directs. There is no safer or more fulfilling place than the center of God's will!

Father, I am thankful to know You will direct me to the center of Your will so I may fulfill it!
Amen!

DAY 49

The Holy Spirit Guides
Us into Truth

However, when He, the Spirit of truth, has come, He will guide you into all truth; for He will not speak on His own authority, but whatever He hears He will speak; and He will tell you things to come.

(John 16:13)

In John, Chapter 16, Jesus is teaching His disciples concerning the work of the Holy Spirit. Earlier in His teaching, He said to them, *"But the Helper, the Holy Spirit, whom the Father will send in My name, He will teach you all things, and bring to your remembrance all things that I said to you"* (John 14:26). We understand the Holy Spirit is a teacher. In addition, in today's verse (quoted above), Jesus referred to the Holy Spirit as *"the Spirit of truth"* who will *"guide you into all truth."* A guide doesn't do everything for you; he just leads you. The Holy Spirit will teach us and lead us, but we have to put forth the effort to believe and study in order to assimilate truth for ourselves. As we read and study to gain understanding, we must trust the Holy Spirit is leading us into truth.

During this same teaching to His disciples, Jesus also said in John 17:17, *"Sanctify them by Your truth. Your word is truth."* Based upon the three references I am quoting in today's devotion, we understand the Holy Spirit is given to us specifically to give revelation knowledge of God's Word. As we read and study the Bible or even as we hear preachers preaching the Word, the Holy Spirit is with us to lead us and guide us into revealed truth.

Notice how John 16:13 ends, *"... He will tell you things to come."* Here Jesus revealed that the Holy Spirit will show us **things to come.** Foreknowledge is a distinct characteristic of God alone. Isaiah 42:9 says, *"Behold, the former things have come to pass, and new things I declare; before they spring forth I tell you of them."* As part of the Godhead, it is the Holy Spirit's role to make this foreknowledge available to the believer. This does not happen automatically for every Christian, but every Spirit-filled believer should know this is available to them to appropriate by faith. This is one of the most miraculous and beneficial ministries of the Holy Spirit and one of the least used. It should be a great joy for you to know the Holy Spirit is with you to lead and guide you in these ways!

Father, I praise You today that the Holy Spirit ministers to me in these ways!
Amen!

DAY 50

Demonstration of the Spirit and Power

And my speech and my preaching were not with persuasive
words of human wisdom, but in demonstration of the Spirit
and of power, that your faith should not be in the wisdom of
men but in the power of God.

(1 Corinthians 2:4–5)

The great Apostle Paul makes a very important point in today's scripture verse which is often overlooked by many modern ministers. It is a common belief among some that miracles
have passed away, or they were only for the early Church until
the establishment of the Church or until we received the written Word of God. The great mistake of the Church today is that
she has a form of godliness but denies the power thereof! (2
Timothy 3:5). This is contrary to what the Bible teaches. Notice,
1 Corinthians 4:20, *"For the kingdom of God is not in word but in*
power." Paul didn't just preach doctrine to attempt to establish
the kingdom of God. The gospel was preached by demonstrating what he taught through the supernatural power of the Holy
Spirit! His message was validated with miraculous signs and

wonders! If Paul needed his message validated with power, how much more does the modern Church need the confirming signs accompanying our message?

The gospel message Paul preached was not with *"persuasive words of human wisdom."* No, his message was accompanied by a *"demonstration of the Spirit and of power."* **This should be the pattern for all true ministers of the gospel!** The majority of the latter half of the Book of Acts focuses on the travels of the Apostle Paul and the spread of the gospel to the Gentiles. Documented for us in that important book are the many miraculous occurrences that happened through his ministry. If we consider the Book of Acts to be more than simply a historical record, but to have significant, theological purpose, we must recognize the value and need for the miraculous in the true preaching of the gospel! The gospel was preached along with powerful demonstration of the Holy Spirit!

The purpose and end result are *"...that your faith should not be in the wisdom of men but in the power of God."* One of the reasons the message which some preach is not more effective is because it is only intellectual, often void of the power of God in the words which are spoken. We **need** the demonstration of the Spirit in our lives. If you will believe for it and be open to it, you will see more of it!

Father, my faith is not in human wisdom but in the demonstration of Your Spirit and power!

Amen!

DAY 51

The Power of the Highest

And the angel answered and said to her, "The Holy Spirit will come upon you, and the power of the Highest will over-shadow you; therefore, also, that Holy One who is to be born will be called the Son of God."

(Luke 1:35)

Luke, Chapter 1, records for us the announcement of Jesus' birth to Mary by the angel Gabriel. Luke 1:26–27 tells us, *"Now in the sixth month the angel Gabriel was sent by God to a city of Galilee named Nazareth, to a virgin betrothed to a man whose name was Joseph, of the house of David. The virgin's name was Mary."* The power of God, through the working of the Holy Spirit, had come to Mary! Today I want you to consider the *"power of the Highest"*. We are told the Holy Spirit came upon the virgin Mary, and the power of the Highest overshadowed her.

This means Mary had found favor with God and the almighty power of God came upon her and the virgin conceived! (vs. 30–31). When the Holy Spirit overshadowed her, the power of the Highest, that is the almighty power of God, performed this miraculous conception! Now, let's consider this amazing fact—**the One with unlimited power dwells in us by the presence of the Holy Spirit within us!**

In Romans, Chapter 8, Paul, writing about walking in the Spirit, not after the flesh (vs. 5), made the amazing statement in verse 11, *"But if the Spirit of Him who raised Jesus from the dead dwells in you, He who raised Christ from the dead will also give life to your mortal bodies through His Spirit who dwells in you."* As Spirit-filled Christians, the same Spirit that raised Jesus from the dead dwells in us! Just as Mary's response to Gabriel's announcement was *"for with God nothing will be impossible"* (Luke 1:37), we should respond likewise!

It should be a great encouragement to know we are not destined to live our lives facing the many challenges life presents in the weakness of our flesh. The Holy Spirit is with us. His power is for us and on our behalf. We are in relationship with God *"by which have been given to us exceedingly great and precious promises"* (2 Peter 1:4). We can access His power by taking hold of the promises by faith. There are no impossible situations with our God. When we face seemingly impossible situations, we should believe for and access the power of the Highest, which will enable us to overcome!

Heavenly Father, I believe Your almighty power is available to me. I will access it by faith and receive Your promises!
Amen!

DAY 52

Strengthened with Might through His Spirit

For this reason I bow my knees to the Father of our Lord Jesus Christ, from whom the whole family in heaven and earth is named, that He would grant you, according to the riches of His glory, to be strengthened with might through His Spirit in the inner man,

(Ephesians 3:14–16)

The Apostle Paul prayed two prayers for the believers in the Book of Ephesians. The first is found in Ephesians 1:15–23, and the second in Chapter 3:14–21. They are both similar in content as he is praying for them to receive a revelation of the mystery he is sharing with them. His writing in the Book of Ephesians is a doctrinal masterpiece packed with spiritual truth, which helps us immensely! These two prayers in Ephesians are sometimes referred to as "epistle prayers," which we can actually personalize and pray for ourselves. Being Spirit-inspired prayers, they are anointed by God Himself and guaranteed to be answered!

In verse 16 of today's scripture, Paul prayed the believers would be *"strengthened with might through His Spirit in the inner man."* There is a great lesson to be learned from this. Many of us, as well-meaning Christians, fall quite short of what God wants for us. The key to all victory in the Christian life is learning how to depend upon the Holy Spirit for our strength. Often, we Christians want to live a life that God desires for us by attempting to live for God instead of allowing God to live through us.

Those who are not born again will never successfully live a Christian life because they do not have God dwelling on the inside of them. Even Christians will fall short of the desired victory without dependence upon the Holy Spirit. Living the Christian life in your own human strength is not just a hard thing to do, it is an impossible thing to do! Are you kidding me? Forgive seventy times seven (Matthew 18:21–22) or when slapped on the cheek in persecution, turn the other cheek also? (Luke 6:29). **All power for the believer originates from the Holy Spirit!**

This prayer ends with Ephesians 3:20, *"Now to Him who is able to do exceedingly abundantly above all that we ask or think, according to the power that works in us."* Notice, this power of the Holy Spirit is not out in the spirit realm somewhere, no, it works in us! Our born-again spirit has already been strengthened. Our challenge is to learn to allow the Holy Spirit's power to manifest in our character!

Heavenly Father, I am thankful You strengthen us with might by Your Spirit in our inner man!
Amen!

DAY 53

The Holy Spirit Witnesses to Us

For by one offering He has perfected forever those who are being sanctified. But the Holy Spirit also witnesses to us; for after He had said before, "This is the covenant that I will make with them after those days, says the Lord: I will put My laws into their hearts, and in their minds I will write them,"

(Hebrews 10:14–16)

These are really great verses that will help us gain an accurate view of the role of the Holy Spirit in our lives! Notice the author of Hebrews is speaking of the offering Jesus made for us (vs. 14). That one sacrifice made by our Lord Jesus has laid the foundation for the eternal sanctification for all who receive it by faith! Then the next sentence says, *"the Holy Spirit also witnesses to us."* This is speaking of the role of the Holy Spirit in the life of every believer!

Many people have the mistaken idea that the Holy Spirit is bringing conviction and condemnation to us every time we do something wrong. They seem to think every time they feel bad or have feelings of self-condemnation or unworthiness, these come from the Holy Spirit. But this does not line up with what the Bible teaches us about the role of the Holy Spirit. The word "witnesses" in today's passage (vs.15) literally means in the original text to "give evidence, or to give a good, honest report, or to give testimony."[4] Many believers actually think it is the Holy Spirit making them feel condemned when in actuality, it is their conscience.

> *And by this we know that we are of the truth, and shall assure our hearts before Him. For if our heart condemns us, God is greater than our heart, and knows all things.*
>
> (1 John 3:19–20)

The Holy Spirit is with you to encourage you and to constantly remind and assure you of God's love for you in spite of the mistakes you have made. He will continually witness to us and remind us, "'*This is the covenant that I will make with them after those days, says the Lord: I will put My laws into their hearts, and in their minds I will write them,' then He adds, 'Their sins and their lawless deeds I will remember no more*'" (Hebrews 10:16–17)! The Holy Spirit is the most important, loving, kind, and powerful person in your life! If you have not understood this about Him, I pray you will change the way you think about Him today.

Father, I love the Holy Spirit and am so thankful for Him! Amen!

---

4 "Strong's Greek: 3140, Μαρτυρέω (Martureó)" (Bible Hub, 2021), https://biblehub.com/greek/3140.htm.

DAY 54

The Holy Spirit is Our Helper

And I will pray the Father, and He will give you another Helper, that He may abide with you forever—the Spirit of truth, whom the world cannot receive, because it neither sees Him nor knows Him; but you know Him, for He dwells with you and will be in you.

(John 14:16–17)

Some refer to John, Chapters 14 through 17, as Jesus' "Farewell Discourse" given to His disciples the night before His arrest, false trial, and crucifixion. In these passages, He prepares His disciples for His going away and promises the Holy Spirit's guidance and help for them. It is important to see how Jesus described the Holy Spirit. He said, *"...I will pray the Father, and He will give you another Helper..."* (vs. 16) or *"Comforter"* as is used in the KJV.

The terminology is significant; He didn't say the Holy Spirit was sent to convict, condemn, or afflict us. He actually said the Holy Spirit would be *"another"* Helper/Comforter. The word "another" literally means "One besides, another of the same kind.[5]

---

5 "Strong's Greek: 243" (Bible Hub, 2021), https://biblehub.com/greek/243.htm.

It was important that Jesus would go away so He could send the Holy Spirit to us as the same kind of Helper/Comforter Jesus is! Jesus was not condemning during His earthly ministry. This is brought out clearly from John 3:17–19,

> *For God did not send His Son into the world to condemn the world, but that the world through Him might be saved. "He who believes in Him is not condemned; but he who does not believe is condemned already, because he has not believed in the name of the only begotten Son of God. And this is the condemnation, that the light has come into the world, and men loved darkness rather than light, because their deeds were evil.*

In His final ministry to His disciples, He said, *"Nevertheless I tell you the truth. It is to your advantage that I go away; for if I do not go away, the Helper will not come to you; but if I depart, I will send Him to you"* (John 16:7). Jesus actually said it is better for us to have the Holy Spirit present with us than to have Jesus Himself physically with us!

The Holy Spirit is not focused on our faults and failures, convicting and condemning us every time we make a mistake or fail Him in some way. No, the Holy Spirit is with us to help, comfort, strengthen, and encourage us in our walk with our God! Hallelujah!

Father, I am thankful and rejoice because Jesus has sent us the Holy Spirit to help and comfort us, not condemn us!
Amen!

DAY 55

The Holy Spirit Draws Us to Jesus

"Nevertheless I tell you the truth. It is to your advantage that I go away; for if I do not go away, the Helper will not come to you; but if I depart, I will send Him to you. And when He has come, He will convict the world of sin, and of righteousness, and of judgment: of sin, because they do not believe in Me."

(John 16:7–9)

There should be no doubt in our minds that the ministry the Holy Spirit brings in the lives of believers is a positive ministry of comfort and help based upon John 16:7. However, many people have been taught to believe the Holy Spirit is the One who makes us feel guilty when we sin or fail and make mistakes. It is common to hear Christians say the Holy Spirit is convicting them of the sin in their lives.

To help us gain a Scriptural perspective of this, let's look closely at what Jesus said in John 16:8–9, *"And when He (Holy Spirit) has come, He (Holy Spirit) will convict the **world of sin**, and of righteousness, and of judgment: **of sin, because they do not believe in***

Me (Jesus)" (emphasis mine). Jesus clearly said the Holy Spirit would convict the world of sin... not believers! What sin is He convicting the world of? The singular sin of not believing in Jesus! This actually takes us right back to the Holy Spirit's role as the Helper. **He's trying to help sinners not go to hell!** People don't go to hell because they sin. Jesus has already dealt with the sins of the whole world, *"And He Himself is the propitiation for our sins, and not for ours only but also for the whole world"* (1 John 2:2). People go to hell because they have a sin nature; they **are** a sinner. The way to change the condition is to believe on the Lord Jesus (Acts 16:31) and what He has done for us!

Even after being born again, it's not our actions (sins) that is the problem. Technically, it is the heart attitude of not trusting in Jesus, which is the root of all sin. This is what the Holy Spirit deals with us about... trusting in Jesus! If we fail to understand this, it will affect the way we relate to God. God is for us; He does not want to judge us or condemn us (John 3:17). We can turn to Him and even receive from Him when we have sinned. There is forgiveness for all!

Father, I am so thankful for the loving, drawing acceptance of Your Spirit in my life. I praise You for it.
Amen!

DAY 56

The Holy Spirit Imparts Life and Truth

It is the Spirit who gives life; the flesh profits nothing. The words that I speak to you are spirit, and they are life.

(John 6:63)

John, Chapter 6, verses 22 through 59, contain what is commonly referred to as The Bread of Life Discourse—a teaching which Jesus delivered in the Synagogue in Capernaum. The discourse contained some hard sayings which offended some of the listeners and even some of His disciples. The Jews who were listening to him were only thinking in the natural realm and were unable to understand the spiritual truth Jesus was attempting to convey. 1 Corinthians 2:14 says,

But the natural man does not receive the things of the Spirit of God, for they are foolishness to him; nor can he know them, because they are spiritually discerned.

Today's verse (quoted above) was Jesus' response to those who murmured against Him and some even *"walked with Him* no more" (vs. 66). Those people were so dominated by their natural, physical existence they missed the whole point Jesus was making, *"For those who live according to the flesh set their minds on the things of the flesh, but those who live according to the Spirit, the things of the Spirit"* (Romans 8:5). Jesus makes a very significant point in today's verse showing, *"The words that I speak to you are spirit, and they are life"*.

1 John 5:7 tells us, *"For there are three that bear witness in heaven: the Father, the Word, and the Holy Spirit; and these three are one."* The Father, the Word (Jesus, John 1:1), and the Holy Spirit will always agree. If we want to know what spiritual truth is, we must believe the Bible, *"All Scripture is given by inspiration of God, and is profitable for doctrine, for reproof, for correction, for instruction in righteousness"* (2 Timothy 3:16). **The written Word of God is inspired by the Holy Spirit. It is spirit and life!** *"For prophecy never came by the will of man, but holy men of God spoke as they were moved by the Holy Spirit"* (2 Peter 1:21). The Bible was written by men who were inspired by the Holy Spirit; therefore, it is an accurate representation of God, Jesus, and the Holy Spirit! We can trust it implicitly and receive an impartation of spirit and life as we read it and understand it. Fully expect the Spirit of God to minister life to you from the living Word of God!

Father, I believe Your Word is spirit and imparts life to me and represents You perfectly!

Amen!

DAY 57

If Anyone Thirsts Let Him Come to Me

On the last day, that great day of the feast, Jesus stood and cried out, saying, "If anyone thirsts, let him come to Me and drink. He who believes in Me, as the Scripture has said, out of his heart will flow rivers of living water." But this He spoke concerning the Spirit, whom those believing in Him would receive; for the Holy Spirit was not yet given, because Jesus was not yet glorified.

(John 7:37–39)

This took place on the last day of the Feast of Tabernacles, which was one of three major festivals observed by the Jewish people. The festival rose to a grand conclusion on the last day when the priest would take a golden pitcher filled with water from the pool of Siloam to the steps of the Temple altar. He would ceremonially ascend the steps declaring Isaiah, Chapter 12. At the top of the steps, he would pour out the water as the highlight of the celebration and declare,

"Cry out and shout, O inhabitant of Zion, for great is the Holy One of Israel in your midst!"

(Isaiah 12:6)

At that very moment, Jesus cried out with a loud voice, *"If anyone thirsts, let him come to Me and drink!"* (John 7:37). Imagine Jesus shouting as He publicly proclaimed to the tens of thousands present, He was the fulfillment of all the ceremony typified! This was so powerful because the priest had just declared from Isaiah 12:6,

"...for great is the Holy One of Israel in your midst!"

John gives the explanation of this in verse 39, *"But this He spoke concerning the Spirit, whom those believing in Him would receive; for the Holy Spirit was not yet given, because Jesus was not yet glorified."* John, writing under the inspiration of the Holy Spirit, interpreted the words of Jesus to refer to the outpouring of the Holy Spirit, which was yet to come on the Day of Pentecost! **Soon the fullness of the Spirit would be a blessing all of God's people could experience!** Notice John wrote, *"whom those believing in Him would receive."* Another confirmation to us the Holy Spirit is given as a gift to the Church, that is, those who believe on Jesus!

The following verses (vs. 40–42) go on to show the people were excited about this. We should be excited about the opportunity to drink of this living water to fill and flow out of our hearts as well!

Father, it excites me to know that the thirsty can come to Jesus to drink of the living water and be filled with the Holy Spirit!
Amen!

DAY 58

We Are the Temple of the Holy Spirit

Or do you not know that your body is the temple of the Holy Spirit who is in you, whom you have from God, and you are not your own? For you were bought at a price; therefore glorify God in your body and in your spirit, which are God's.

(1 Corinthians 6:19–20)

It is interesting the Holy Spirit inspired Paul, who was the author of 1 Corinthians, to use the phrase *"temple of the Holy Spirit."* The Corinthians were Greek and were accustomed to the Greek culture their whole lives. The temples of the Greeks were beautiful structures with marble columns, granite floors, hand-carved woodwork, and gold overlay. The use of the word "temple" to describe our born-again spirit is very significant!

Jesus likewise used the term Himself when He was questioned by the Jews for His first cleansing of the Jewish Temple, *"So the Jews answered and said to Him, 'What sign do You show to us, since You do these things?' Jesus answered and said to them, 'Destroy this temple, and in three days I will raise it up'"* (John 2:18–19). The Jews thought He spoke of Herod's Temple, which was a beautiful and magnificent structure that had been under construction for forty-six years, but He spoke of the temple of His body (vs. 21).

When we are born again by confessing Jesus as our Lord and Savior, our spirit is instantly created as a magnificent habitation for the Holy Spirit to dwell within us! Jesus said in John 14:17, *"the Spirit of truth, whom the world cannot receive, because it neither sees Him nor knows Him; but you know Him, **for He dwells with you and will be in you.**"* This stands in stark contrast to the believers in Old Testament times. Old Testament believers could not be born again because Jesus had not yet been to the cross. So, the Holy Spirit could not dwell in them because they were not a suitable habitation for Him. The Holy Spirit would come upon the prophet, priest, and king to enable them to do a job and then lift from them.

As new creatures created in Christ Jesus (2 Corinthians 5:17), **we have become a suitable habitation for the Spirit and are now the dwelling place of God!** We are not a dirty, unworthy shack unfit for the presence of the Spirit of God. Because of the grace of God, the fruit of the Spirit, the gifts of the Spirit, and God's workmanship, our spirit has become a magnificent dwelling place for the Spirit of God to dwell!

Heavenly Father, I rejoice and welcome the constant presence of Your Spirit within me!
Amen!

DAY 59

The Fruit of the Spirit in You

But the fruit of the Spirit is love, joy, peace, longsuffering, kindness, goodness, faithfulness, gentleness, self-control. Against such there is no law.

(Galatians 5:22–23)

I recently met a man who has been incarcerated for nearly twenty years. Every time I see him, he is smiling, and there is joy evident in his life. When he told me he has been down so long, I said, "Wow, that's a long time!" He said, "It is a long time, but I am free." He's not free on the outside, but he is free on the inside!

He's been developing his relationship with the Lord over the last few years. Although he hasn't been saved a long time, I believe he is demonstrating genuine growth in his life, evidenced by the fruit he is producing. True Christianity comes from the inside out. Matthew 12:33–35 records Jesus' words about this subject,

"Either make the tree good and its fruit good, or else make the tree bad and its fruit bad; for a tree is known by its fruit... For out of the abundance of the heart the mouth speaks. A good man out of the good treasure of his heart brings forth good things, and an evil man out of the evil treasure brings forth evil things."

A good tree does not produce bad fruit, neither does a bad tree produce good fruit. Fruit comes forth from the root. If the root is corrupt, the fruit will be corrupt. Experiencing life with joy, peace, gentleness, goodness, and self-control begins with a decision that affects the root or core of man.

Lasting fruit is not obtained through behavior modification. A good heart will change a man's actions, but a man's actions cannot change his heart. Someone may reason that a man who has lost his physical freedom and has spent so many years in prison couldn't possibly have joy. This reasoning assumes the fruit in our lives is only connected to the circumstances of life. **The fruit of the Spirit is abundant in our born-again spirit, but it is not automatically manifested in our lives. It must be appropriated by faith.** Know today a good, fruitful life is available to you. Make the decision which affects your root and begin to enjoy the fruitful life!

Father God, thank you for making me free! Thank you for the fruit of the Spirit in my life.
Amen!

DAY 60

Sealed with the Holy Spirit

In Him you also trusted, after you heard the word of truth, the gospel of your salvation; in whom also, having believed, you were sealed with the Holy Spirit of promise,

(Ephesians 1:13)

This verse makes an important statement to us, *"having believed, you were sealed with the Holy Spirit of promise."* As believers, we have been "sealed" with the Holy Spirit. The word "sealed" is translated from a word in the original Greek text which means "to stamp (with a signet or private mark) for security or preservation, to attest, or seal up."[6] This communicates a very important truth to us. This is communicating to us that **the Holy Spirit is protecting our salvation once we have believed!**

Notice this verse mentions two requirements that must take place before this sealing can occur:

1. the gospel must be heard, and
2. the gospel must be believed and trusted.

---

6 "Strong's #4972" (Bible Tools, 2021), https://www.bibletools.org/index.cfm/fuseaction/Lexicon.show/ID/G4972/sphragizo.htm.

Preaching is the chosen method God has given for communicating His Gospel message, *"How then shall they call on Him in whom they have not believed? And how shall they believe in Him of whom they have not heard? And how shall they hear without a preacher?"* (Romans 10:14). Once a person has heard the Gospel, it must be believed and trusted by acting on it by faith,

> *that if you confess with your mouth the Lord Jesus and believe in your heart that God has raised Him from the dead, you will be saved. For with the heart one believes unto righteousness, and with the mouth confession is made unto salvation.*
>
> (Romans 10:9–10)

At salvation, a person's spirit becomes a new creation (2 Corinthians 5:17) which is free from sin and totally pure. According to today's verse (quoted above), the believer's spirit is immediately "sealed". A barrier is formed to keep sin out, so the spirit man retains purity! When a Christian sins, it is in the physical and soulish realm; the spirit does not participate. 1 John 3:9 states,

> *Whoever has been born of God does not sin, for His seed remains in him; and he cannot sin, because he has been born of God.*

This means as a believer in Jesus, our salvation is secure! It is a common belief among some that sin can actually cause us to lose our salvation, but the Bible does not teach this. We have been saved and sanctified, and sin cannot affect our relationship with God! It does affect your relationship with the devil, however! So, if you are sinning, stop it!

Heavenly Father, I have believed and trusted in the Gospel. I believe I am secure in You!

Amen!

DAY 61

Do Not Grieve the Holy Spirit

And do not grieve the Holy Spirit of God, by whom you were sealed for the day of redemption.

(Ephesians 4:30)

Some might argue, "If God is not holding our sin against us, and if sin does not affect our relationship with God, why resist sin?" It is true God is not holding sin against us, but don't take my word for it. Romans 5:13 tells us, *"For until the law sin was in the world, but sin is not imputed when there is no law,"* as well as 2 Corinthians 5:19, *"that is, that God was in Christ reconciling the world to Himself, not imputing their trespasses to them..."* It is true sin is not being imputed to us during this dispensation of Grace, but there are two valid reasons for not living in sin.

First, **God is not holding your sin against you, but the devil is!** When you live in sin it opens the door to the devil to come into your life to kill, steal, and destroy (John 10:10). Sin doesn't affect your relationship with God, but it sure is affecting your relationship with the devil! If you don't want him to kill, steal, and destroy your life... shut the door on him by resisting sin!

The second reason a believer should want to resist sin is that it grieves the Holy Spirit. The Holy Spirit is a person, and it is possible for us to grieve Him. The word "grieve" in today's verse is translated from a Greek word which means "to distress, to be sad, to be in heaviness, to make sorry."[7] The word would describe a pain or grief which could only be caused by two people who love each other deeply. If a husband or wife is unfaithful to the other, the betrayed spouse feels a sense of shock, hurt, or devastation and pain associated with the unfaithfulness.

The Holy Spirit loves us deeply. When a child of God chooses to live in open sin, the Holy Spirit is "grieved" by those acts. He experiences distress, sadness, heaviness, and sorrow. The Holy Spirit loves and cherishes us. Because He dwells in us, we drag Him into the sin with us when we go there through our actions. That is when/how we grieve Him.

God will never leave nor forsake us (Hebrews 13:5), and His love and commitment to us are unfailing. There is nothing we can do to make Him love us less, but we can grieve Him with wrong actions.

Father, thank you for Your unfailing love and commitment to me even when I fail!
Amen!

---

7 "Strong's Greek: 3076" (Bible Hub, 2021), https://biblehub.com/greek/3076.htm.

DAY 62

The Holy Spirit is God

But Peter said, "Ananias, why has Satan filled your heart to lie to the Holy Spirit and keep back part of the price of the land for yourself? While it remained, was it not your own? And after it was sold, was it not in your own control? Why have you conceived this thing in your heart? You have not lied to men but to God."

(Acts 5:3–4)

The judgment leveled against Ananias and Sapphira is a most intriguing story recorded in Acts, Chapter 5. The early Church had developed a system of communal living where everyone involved *"had all things in common"* (Acts 2:44). We can see this sharing was totally voluntary based upon Peter's comment in Acts 5:4, *"While it remained, was it not your own? And after it was sold, was it not in your own control?"* So, there was nothing wrong with Ananias and Sapphira selling their land; the issue was, they lied about it. Peter asked them,

"...why has Satan filled your heart to lie to the Holy Spirit..."

Their hypocrisy and dishonesty were not only to the other members of the church, but Peter said to them, *"You have not lied to men but to God"* (vs. 4). Peter plainly stated in verse 4 they had lied to the Holy Spirit; then in verse 5, he said they had lied to God. **This is one of the clearest references in all of Scripture, showing the Holy Spirit is God!** This shows us clearly that we should honor the Holy Spirit, His presence, and guidance the same way we would honor God Himself!

Another verse supporting this thought is 1 John 5:7, *"For there are three that bear witness in heaven: the Father, the Word, and the Holy Spirit; and these three are one."* God, Himself, is in us and works with us and through us by the Holy Spirit dwelling in us. As we learn to discern and follow the voice of the Holy Spirit within us, we can be confident it is God's voice to us and His help working to lead us. Jesus taught us the same,

> *"These things I have spoken to you while being present with you. But the Helper, the Holy Spirit, whom the Father will send in My name, He will teach you all things, and bring to your remembrance all things that I said to you."*
>
> (John 14:25–26)

Heavenly Father, I honor the Holy Spirit just as I honor You. I want to hear and follow the leading of Your Spirit, and as I do, I am confident I am following You!

Amen!

DAY 63

The Holy Spirit Helps in Our Weakness

Likewise the Spirit also helps in our weaknesses. For we do not know what we should pray for as we ought, but the Spirit Himself makes intercession for us with groanings which cannot be uttered. Now He who searches the hearts knows what the mind of the Spirit is, because He makes intercession for the saints according to the will of God.

(Romans 8:26–27)

I have previously made the point when one receives the baptism with the Holy Spirit, he/she is supernaturally given the ability to speak in other tongues. This is a language you were not taught and did not learn on your own; it is an initial evidence one has truly received the baptism with the Holy Spirit.

We have all experienced times when we do not know how to pray as we ought simply because we are limited in our knowledge and by our finite brains. This verse tells us the *"Spirit also helps in our weaknesses."* The word *"helps"* is translated from a Greek word which literally means "to take hold of opposite together."[8] This communicates a powerful truth to us. When we are praying and come to the place when we no longer know what to say or to pray as we ought, the Holy Spirit will help us by making intercession for us or with us! When we shift over into praying in the Spirit (1 Corinthians 14:15–17), by praying in another tongue, the Holy Spirit actually "takes hold of opposite together" with us by shouldering the load to help us move the mountain we are praying about!

In the natural, you may not know all the details of the situation, but the Spirit of God does! Verse 27 says, *"He makes intercession for the saints according to the will of God."* When you begin to pray in the Spirit, you can be confident you are praying the perfect will of God! When your understanding is exhausted, the Holy Spirit makes up the difference. There are only two kinds of problems you can have—the kind when you don't know how to pray and the kind when you do know how to pray. If you do know what to pray, pray with your understanding; if you don't know what to pray, pray in the Spirit, knowing the Holy Spirit is helping you pray the perfect will of God! With the Holy Spirit as your intercessor, you can't lose. If you have not yet received the Holy Spirit baptism, with the evidence of praying in other tongues, pray the prayer at the end of this book to receive!

Father, I'm thankful to know Your Spirit intercedes through me! Amen!

---

8 "Strong's #4878" (Bible Tools, 2021), https://www.bibletools.org/index.cfm/fuseaction/Lexicon.show/ID/G4878/sunantilambanomai.htm.

DAY 64

Revelation through His Spirit

But as it is written: "Eye has not seen, nor ear heard, nor have entered into the heart of man the things which God has prepared for those who love Him." But God has revealed them to us through His Spirit. For the Spirit searches all things, yes, the deep things of God.

(1 Corinthians 2:9–10)

This is a familiar verse to many who love to think about all God has prepared for those of us who love Him. No doubt our God does have some fantastic things for us to enjoy in eternity! In addition, Paul is emphasizing the impossibility of mankind understanding God's wisdom through their own natural mental capacity. But those of us who love God and are born again are not limited to our own natural mental abilities. Our God has actually made it possible for His people to access His wisdom.

This is brought out in verse 10 of today's passage, *"But God has revealed them to us through His Spirit."* It is true no man has ever perceived, in his natural ability, the things prepared for us by God. But this does not mean we cannot receive revelation from God through His Word and by His Spirit! Jesus actually taught in John 6:45 that this was foreseen by Old Testament prophets, *"It is written in the prophets, 'And they shall all be taught by God.' Therefore everyone who has heard and learned from the Father comes to Me."* The Old Testament prophets prophesied of a New Covenant where we would be taught by God (Jeremiah 31:31–34; Isaiah 54:13). Under the Old Testament, God dealt with man through the outer man because they were incapable of being born again before Jesus went to the cross.

But as New Testament believers, we can be born again and perceive New Covenant truths revealed to us by His Spirit. *"Now we have received, not the spirit of the world, but the Spirit who is from God, that we might know the things that have been freely given to us by God. These things we also speak, not in words which man's wisdom teaches but which the Holy Spirit teaches, comparing spiritual things with spiritual"* (1 Corinthians 2:12–13). One of the greatest evidences of having received the baptism with the Holy Spirit is the great amount of God's wisdom, which is available to us! I encourage you today to be more aware of the dealings of the Spirit of God. I'm confident He wants to reveal more of His Word and His desire to accomplish a great work in you!

Father, I am thankful You make revelation available by Your Spirit! Amen!

DAY 65

Encouraged by the Spirit

Then the church throughout Judea, Galilee and Samaria
enjoyed a time of peace and was strengthened. Living in the
fear of the Lord and encouraged by the Holy Spirit, it in-
creased in numbers.

(Acts 9:31 NIV)

As a result of the conversion of Saul of Tarsus on the road to
Damascus (Acts 9:3–5), the persecution against the Church was
greatly reduced. Saul of Tarsus was a religious terrorist bent
on destroying the Church of the Lord Jesus. Saul was radically saved and changed by the experience and, not wasting any
time, *"Immediately he preached the Christ in the synagogues, that He*
is the Son of God" (Acts 9:20). Saul (who became Paul) was able to
effectively preach Jesus and communicate the Gospel of Grace,
which resulted in strength and peace being imparted to the
churches.

This ministry of the Gospel of Grace being preached within
the Church throughout Judea, Galilee, and Samaria, enabled
the Holy Spirit to accomplish a work of encouragement in the
believers. Paul the Apostle mentioned the same thing in his

closing remarks in his epistle to the Romans, *"Now may the God of hope fill you with all joy and peace in believing, that you may abound in hope by the power of the Holy Spirit"* (Romans 15:13). Paul makes this reference to the God of hope, which is another beautiful name for our God, asking Him to fill these believers with joy and peace in believing.

As these believers trusted in God, their faith brought joy and peace to their hearts *"that you may abound in hope by the power of the Holy Spirit."* Paul is referencing more than a natural human hopefulness; he is suggesting a supernatural, **Holy Spirit-powered hopefulness and encouragement to operate within them as they believe!** The Holy Spirit is able to minister encouragement to you in the form of peace, joy, security, and hopeful expectation, but you have a part to play in receiving this encouragement. You must believe the Gospel of Grace and exercise faith, which cooperates with what God has done for us! The Word of God has been inspired by the Holy Spirit and given to us to strengthen and build us up!

I trust these devotions on the ministry of the precious Holy Spirit are blessing you and helping you to grasp a better realization of His presence and work within us all. Receive the encouragement of the Holy Spirit as He is with you helping, comforting, and strengthening you!

Father, I appreciate so much the encouraging presence of the Holy Spirit with me constantly. I rely on You, and I believe You will confirm it daily!

Amen!

Part Three:

THE BENEFITS OF HIS GRACE

Introduction

The devotions in this section entitled The Benefits of His Grace are dedicated to discussing some of the important benefits we have as Christians, which have been provided to us by our Heavenly Father. Psalm 103:2 says, *"Bless the Lord, O my soul, and forget not all His benefits."* The reason we are told not to forget is that we will forget if we do not make a conscious effort to remember!

There are many, many things God has done for us and made available to help us in our Christian lives. It will be good for you to read these daily devotions, which will remind you of the good things God has done for you. Some of them are quite obvious, but there may be some things that are new thoughts for you. I hope as you read, you will sense gratefulness to God rise in your heart for the many benefits He has provided for you. Be sure to express your thankfulness and praise to Him after reading each one. I pray this will bless you as you read.

—Chaplain McComb

DAY 66

Forget Not All His Benefits

Bless the Lord, O my soul; and all that is within me, bless His holy name! Bless the Lord, O my soul, and forget not all His benefits.

(Psalm 103:1–2)

It is interesting the psalmist David makes the special effort to speak to his soul and everything within him, commanding it to *"Bless the Lord (...) bless His holy name!"* I don't know the specific issues David was dealing with in his mind and emotions when he wrote this, but I can relate to times in my own life when I have felt despair, anxiety, or fear trying to take over my thoughts. I would imagine everyone reading this could relate in some way or another to wrong thoughts attacking their mind.

It's important at times like those to bring every thought captive (2 Corinthians 10:3–5) and remember the faithfulness and loyalty of God in our lives. We must keep our mind stayed on Him so we experience peace (Isaiah 26:3) rather than the turmoil wrong thinking will produce in our soul.

David then said, *"and forget not all His benefits..."* Yes, there are benefits to serving God! Benefits are not the reason we should serve Him. If there were no more benefit to serving Him other than being saved from hell and given eternal life, this would be more than we deserve and a reason to serve Him the rest of our lives! Some have made statements like, "I wouldn't serve a God who isn't good or one who doesn't bless, or heal, or provide, etc."

I think that is missing the whole point. **We serve God and love Him because He is God and we are not!** If there were no other benefit to serving God at all, we should still love and serve Him. Probably everyone reading this had some selfish motivation for receiving the Lord. I know I did. I didn't want to go to hell! When I fully understood dying without Jesus as Lord of my life meant I would immediately go into a Christ-less eternity that settled it for me.

But, as we can see from this verse, there are benefits to serving our God. Do you know why we are exhorted to *"forget not all His benefits"*? Because **we will forget if we do not make a conscious effort to remember!** Because God is good and loves us supremely, He has included countless benefits to this life with Him. We will explore many of them in this devotional.

Father, I believe there are many benefits to serving You, and I praise You for every one of them!
Amen!

DAY 67

He Forgives All Our Sins

Bless the Lord, O my soul; and all that is within me, bless
His holy name! Bless the Lord, O my soul, and forget not all
His benefits: Who forgives all your iniquities...

(Psalm 103:1–3)

One of the greatest and necessary benefits we receive from God is the forgiveness of our sins! From the beginning of human history, forgiveness of sins was only possible through the shed blood of an acceptable substitute. In the Old Testament, it was the blood of an animal sacrifice that was applied to their lives to produce an atoning of sin, which was only a covering and could not remove their sin (Hebrews 9:15–22), which is why it had to be repeated every year.

Jesus has become our suitable sacrifice, *"so Christ was offered once to bear the sins of many..."* (Hebrews 9:28). The blood of Jesus is what has provided forgiveness of sins for us. His sacrifice was so great that it outweighed all our sins. Not just the sins of the Church but also the sins of the whole world! (1 John 2:2).

Forgiveness of sins is not the ultimate goal of our salvation, but it is a necessary step. The ultimate goal of our salvation is a relationship with God, and sin was a barrier to that relationship. It had to be dealt with, and it was through the blood of Jesus! Colossians 1:14 says, *"In whom we have redemption through His blood, the forgiveness of sins."* When the blood of Jesus is applied to our lives, it doesn't simply cover our sin. No, it removes it totally, so completely that it leaves no stain!

From God's perspective, our sins are removed from us *"as far as the east is from the west..."* (Psalm 103:12). But some who do not understand this still attempt to relate to God with a law-based performance mentality, often carrying a sense of shame and guilt for sins and mistakes they make. Tormented with anxiety, they feel dirty and unworthy to approach God.

God would have you to know that once you received Jesus and asked Him to forgive you, He did! His blood is applied, and there is no need to carry excessive remorse for the sins of the past, which alienates you from the intimate relationship our Father desires to have with you. This tremendous benefit will *"...cleanse your conscience from dead works to serve the living God"* (Hebrews 9:14)!

Father, thank you for forgiving my sin and cleansing my conscience so I may freely serve You without fear and shame!
Amen!

DAY 68

He Heals All Our Diseases

Bless the Lord, O my soul, and forget not all His benefits:
Who forgives all your iniquities, Who heals all your diseases,
(Psalm 103:2–3)

Notice today's scripture mentions forgiveness of iniquities and healing of disease together in one verse. In today's modern culture, it is common for some churches or ministers to accept that God is willing to forgive sins, but they doubt He will heal disease. Forgiveness and healing were never intended by God to be separated. God would no more have you to sin than He would have you to be sick. Many scriptures combine the healing of our bodies and the forgiveness of our sins (e.g., Psalm 103:3; Isaiah 53:4–6; 1 Peter 2:24).

When Jesus went to the cross, He bore the punishment for the sins we committed. As our substitute, He died in our place so forgiveness of sin could come to us. But remember, He also went to the whipping post for us the same day. Matthew 27:26 tells us, *"Then he (Pilate) released Barabbas to them; and when he had scourged Jesus, he delivered Him to be crucified"* (emphasis mine). Scripture tells us the reason Jesus bore stripes at the whipping post, *"who Himself bore our sins in His own body on the tree, that we, having died to sins, might live for righteousness—by whose stripes you were healed"* (1 Peter 2:24).

Jesus bore our sins when He died on the cross and bore stripes on His back at the whipping post for our healing. This means healing is part of the atonement! Healing has been purchased for us in God's redemptive plan and is now offered to us by God's grace to be received by faith. This is another great benefit that our God has made available to us. Many people live far below their rights and privileges because of ignorance or disbelief.

One reason many fail to receive their healing is that they do not know it is God's will to heal all. This is easily settled in our minds with one verse of scripture. *"Who (Jesus) being the brightness of His glory and the express image of His person, and upholding all things by the word of His power, when He had by Himself purged our sins, sat down at the right hand of the Majesty on high"* (Hebrews 1:3, emphasis mine). Jesus is the express image of God's person, which means He is an exact representation of God. Jesus always healed the sick, demonstrating it is always God's will to heal. Know today healing is God's will for you.

Father God, I believe it is Your will to heal all my diseases! Amen!

DAY 69

He Redeems Our Life from Destruction

Who redeems your life from destruction, who crowns you with lovingkindness and tender mercies,

(Psalm 103:4)

The word "destruction" in today's verse literally means "pit" or "corruption," plainly stated in the Amplified version of the Bible,

Who redeems your life from the pit and corruption, who beautifies, dignifies, and crowns you with lovingkindness and tender mercy.

(Psalm 103:4 AMPC)

Jesus purchased redemption for us, but our redemption is not complete yet. When we are born again, one-third of our salvation is complete. When we receive Jesus as Lord and Savior, our spirit is saved, made alive unto God as a new creation (2 Corinthians 5:17). But our soul and body are in process. We are to be transformed by the renewing of our mind (Romans 12:2), which affects our soul. The purchase of our total salvation has already been made by the blood of Jesus, but our bodies are not redeemed yet. One day, after our death, those who are born again will receive their glorified body and be present with the Lord in heaven! (2 Corinthians 5:8).

The ultimate goal of our redemption is not missing hell, although I am thankful for that, amen? We have been redeemed from destruction and crowned with lovingkindness and tender mercies, which is awesome, but the ultimate goal of our redemption is a relationship with God. This is what Jesus said in John 17:3, *"And this is eternal life, that they may know You, the only true God, and Jesus Christ whom You have sent."* Eternal life is not just living forever; it is knowing God and Jesus personally and intimately.

Everyone will exist forever in one of two places. Those who are saved will spend it in heaven with the Lord, those who are lost, in hell, separated from God's presence. Hell was never created for man. The only reason mankind will experience hell is for the sin of rejecting Jesus (John 16:9). **Man does not go to hell because he sins; man goes to hell because he is a sinner. If he does not want to go to hell, he has to change the condition.** How do you do that? Man's individual sins do not create the condition, and lack of sin won't correct it. Jesus said, *"Do not marvel that I said to you, 'You must be born again'"* (John 3:7). We must never forget what David told us here—The Lord is the One who redeems our lives from destruction (Psalm 103:4).

Father, I am thankful You have redeemed my life from destruction. I believe You crown me with lovingkindness and tender mercy.
Amen!

DAY 70

He Renews Our Youth Like the Eagle's

Who satisfies your mouth with good things, So that your youth is renewed like the eagle's.

(Psalm 103:5)

The older I get, the more I appreciate this verse! This is possibly a reference to the annual molting or casting off of the eagle's old feathers to receive new ones which are healthy and strong.

It is true everyone undergoes the aging process. It is only a matter of time until all of us are aged. But here is a promise from God that should be factored into our belief system... *"your youth is renewed"*! It is generally accepted in our culture when one reaches a certain age, they can expect to begin to go "downhill" in their health as the norm. Often birthdays are celebrated by displaying black balloons or jokes about their "memory failing," etc. I understand a lot of this is just done in fun, certainly nothing wrong with joking around with a family member or friend.

But when we begin to believe these things about ourselves and expect them to come to pass, this is a problem! Psalm 91:16 says, *"With long life I will satisfy him, and show him My salvation."* Here is a promise from God of long life. A long life implies a healthy life. If a person isn't healthy, they can't live long. What is a long life? *"The days of our lives are seventy years; and if by reason of strength they are eighty years"* (Psalm 90:10). This should be the minimum number of years we should expect to live. Moses lived to be 120 years old (Deuteronomy 34:7). Psalm 91:16 says God will satisfy us with long life. If you are not satisfied with 70 or 80, then keep going until you are satisfied!

It matters what you believe about this. You can believe and receive or doubt and do without; it's up to you. You should develop your faith based upon what the Bible says, not upon what our culture says or another person's experience. I encourage you to believe you will age gracefully, having your youth renewed like the eagle's. Someone may say, "I don't know if I believe that." Okay, then it won't work for you. As for me, I choose to believe the promises. I don't always do it perfectly, but I'm a believer, not a doubter. You have to choose to abide in Him and let His Word abide in you (John 15:7) to experience God's best.

Father, I thank you today for Your promise of youth renewed and long life satisfied. I believe I receive it.
Amen!

DAY 71

The Kindness and Love of God Appeared to Us

But when the kindness and the love of God our Savior toward man appeared, not by works of righteousness which we have done, but according to His mercy He saved us, through the washing of regeneration and renewing of the Holy Spirit,

(Titus 3:4–5)

We all understand God's redemptive plan for man included the provision of eternal salvation described in today's verse "... *He saved us, through the washing of regeneration and renewing of the Holy Spirit,*" which God accomplished for us by sending His Son when the fullness of time had come (Galatians 4:4). When Jesus came on the scene of humanity, it marked a distinct change in God's dealing with man. God was dealing with man according to the dispensation of the Law of Moses. It was a time when God's wrath was in manifestation. Galatians 4:4 tells us, *"God sent forth His Son, born of a woman, born under the law."* Jesus was born under the law, lived under the law, and fulfilled it perfectly to end God's dealings with man according to the law (Galatians 3:23–24).

I want to point out the truth which today's verse is emphasizing for us, *"But when the **kindness** and the **love** of God our Savior toward man appeared (...) according to His **mercy** He saved us"*. Jesus' substitutionary sacrifice has enabled God to deal with man according to kindness, love, and mercy! This is an awesome benefit of serving God, which we must never forget!

The Law of Moses had a specific purpose (Galatians 3:24), but it was necessary for Jesus to come so God could manifest His fullness to us. *"And of His fullness we have all received, and grace for grace. For the law was given through Moses, but grace and truth came through Jesus Christ"* (John 1:16–17). Jesus didn't come bringing the wrath of God, instead, He brought grace and truth.

We no longer relate to God according to *"works of righteousness which we have done,"* we now relate to Him by faith in His grace. Jesus' appearance changed everything for us. God is now dealing with us strictly by grace. This means He now extends His unfailing love, kindness, and mercy to us at all times, even if, and especially when, we do not deserve it! We all make mistakes at times, and failure to understand this will produce anxiety, dread, and fear. Understanding this truth about God will free you to serve Him without fear.

Father, I am so glad to know Your unfailing love, kindness, and mercy. Thank you for extending Your grace to me at all times!
Amen!

DAY 72

Jesus Bore Our Punishment

And I, if I am lifted up from the earth, will draw all peoples to Myself.

(John 12:32)

We read in John, Chapter 12, that Greeks had come to Jerusalem to worship at the Feast of Passover. They explained to Philip they wanted to see Jesus. Gentiles had come to Jesus at times before to receive a miracle and experience His supernatural power. But this time, it was different. These Greeks came seeking Him to worship Him! When Jesus heard this, it prompted Him to make His comments in verses 23 through 36. He began to say His hour had come and began to speak about His coming death.

He could no longer confine His ministry to the Jews. John 12:26 tells us, *"If anyone serves Me, let him follow Me; and where I am, there My servant will be also. If anyone serves Me, him My Father will honor."* Notice what He didn't say. He didn't say His ministry was not for Gentiles. He said if *"anyone serves Me."* Redemption would also be for the Gentiles! Jesus spoke of what His death would accomplish for us in verses 31 through 32. The sins of the world were about to be placed upon Jesus. God was about to judge sin. Jesus was about to suffer punishment on our behalf!

These verses speak of the death Jesus would die and the judgment/punishment He would suffer. In fact, the word "peoples" is italicized because it was not in the original Greek text; it was added by the translators. Jesus actually said, *"If I am lifted up from the earth, (I) will draw all (...) to Myself"* (vs. 32). All what? All Judgment! He was speaking of the death He would die on the cross. **When He was lifted up on the cross, He actually drew the judgment/punishment for sin on Himself.** Much the way a lightning rod draws a lightning strike, judgment for the sin of the world was placed upon Jesus!

There is no reason for us to fear the judgment of God. The punishment we deserve was placed on Jesus so we can be forgiven and free from the fear of punishment for the things we have done! The price has already been paid by the only One who can pay it! All Jesus asks of us to make redemption complete is to receive it by faith! We should "fear" God in the sense we have a holy reverential awe and respect for Him, but we should not fear Him in the sense we are afraid of Him! He receives us as a good and loving Father!

Heavenly Father, thank you that Jesus has taken the punishment I deserve so I can be forgiven!

Amen!

DAY 73

God Has Made Us Sons

*And because you are sons, God has sent forth the Spirit of
His Son into your hearts, crying out, "Abba, Father!"*

(Galatians 4:6)

Jesus taught us to relate to God as our Father, *"And in that
day you will ask Me nothing. Most assuredly, I say to you, whatever
you ask the Father in My name He will give you"* (John 16:23) and *"In
this manner, therefore, pray: Our Father in heaven, Hallowed be Your
name"* (Matthew 6:9). Although this is common knowledge to
many in Christendom, there are many who do not understand
this. Often, we hear people who begin their prayer "Almighty
God" or "Creator". Of course, God is almighty, and He is the
Creator of the universe, but this is not how the Bible teaches us
as His children to relate to Him.

The Jewish leaders of Jesus' day simply did not have the con-
cept of relating to God as their Father. Although the word "father" was used many times in the Old Testament, it was rarely
used in reference to God. God was referenced as Father on a few
occasions (Isaiah 9:6, 63:16; Jeremiah 3:19) but, the Jews did not
have this understanding. This is seen clearly in John, Chapter

5. When Jesus healed a paralytic at the pool of Bethesda on a Sabbath day, we are told,

> *For this reason the Jews persecuted Jesus, and sought to kill Him, because He had done these things on the Sabbath.*
>
> (John 5:16)

Jesus' response to them was *"'My Father has been working until now, and I have been working.' Therefore the Jews sought all the more to kill Him, because He not only broke the Sabbath, but also said that God was His Father, making Himself equal with God"* (John 5:17–18).

One of the benefits of being God's son is receiving the indwelling of His Spirit (see Galatians 4:6 quoted above). This allows the believer to address God in the same manner Jesus did, *"Abba Father"* (Mark 14:35–36), and carries the idea, God is our daddy. It is a term of affection and fondness! As God's adopted son/daughter, you have the right to His favor, blessing, provision, protection, and all the benefits of relationship as a natural child.

It is a great benefit to those of us who are Christian to be able to relate to God as our Father! He is not our cold, harsh judge. He is our loving, caring, merciful Father with Whom we may have an intimate relationship.

Heavenly Father, I love You and am thankful to be able to address You as Abba Father!

Amen!

DAY 74

God Has Made a Covenant of Peace with Us

For this is like the waters of Noah to Me; for as I have sworn that the waters of Noah would no longer cover the earth, so have I sworn that I would not be angry with you, nor rebuke you. For the mountains shall depart and the hills be removed, but My kindness shall not depart from you, nor shall My covenant of peace be removed," Says the Lord, who has mercy on you.

(Isaiah 54:9–10)

Isaiah, Chapter 53, is one of the most well-known Messianic prophecies of the Old Testament, in which Isaiah prophesied Jesus' suffering and death for the redemption of mankind. Jesus is our substitute; He bore the whole burden of the world's sin and sickness as payment for us! His sin-bearing death was the divine plan, which has brought release to all of God's people.

The suffering of Jesus described in Isaiah, Chapter 53, is the cause of rejoicing in Chapter 54! God was speaking specifically to the Jewish nation, but this also has application to Christians today as we see the unchanging covenant love of God described. The prophet was inspired to write, *"...so have I sworn that I would not be angry with you, nor rebuke you. For the mountains shall depart and the hills be removed, but My kindness shall not depart from you, nor shall My covenant of peace be removed".* Through Jesus's suffering and sacrifice, God has provided a covenant of peace with us!

There are two types of covenants in the Bible:

1. conditional, which depended upon the participation of one or both parties.
2. unconditional, which required no stipulations.

This covenant of peace was likened unto Noah's covenant, *"For this is like the waters of Noah to Me; for as I have sworn that the waters of Noah would no longer cover the earth, so have I sworn..."* Noah's covenant was an unconditional covenant God made in which He promised never again to destroy the earth with a flood.

This covenant of peace in Isaiah 54 is unconditional. We now have the unconditional promise of God guaranteeing the war between God and man is over, including the unfailing love and mercy of God, His strong protection and provision toward us forever! Now, this is good news and one of the greatest benefits there is of being in relationship with our God! What peace and stability it brings to our heart to know this is ours from our Father.

Father, I thank you for the Covenant of peace You have made with me.

Amen!

DAY 75

God is Good

Oh, give thanks to the Lord, for He is good! For His mercy endures forever.

(Psalm 107:1)

Understanding the goodness of God is necessary for all of us. There are so many who do not understand this, and if they did, they would never accuse God of some of the things they do. Here the psalmist emphasizes goodness as the true "essence" and "character" of God. Notice it says *"...for He is good!"*

"Good" is not just a trait God possesses, "Good" is not something God does, "Good" is not just one of His qualities; no, "Good" is what God is! And He cannot be anything else! I'll share a story as an example of what I mean. At the time of this writing, I have been the Chaplain at the Kyle Correctional Center in Kyle, TX, for twenty-two years. I have conducted a weekly Sunday night Chapel service my entire tenure. Every week, I preach from a small, plywood tabletop lectern. Let's say one week I decide to go to Las Vegas for a little R & R (bear with me in a little folly here), partying, womanizing, and gambling. I return home the next Sunday, take my place behind my lectern, and amazingly, it is plywood! My week's performance didn't change it at all!

Now let's say I decide to take another week to seek God in the mountains of Colorado in fasting, prayer, and Bible study. I return home, take my place behind the lectern, and... it's still plywood! The week's performance didn't change it either! Why? Because plywood is what it **is**, and it cannot be anything else. I can't change it. My performance doesn't affect it at all! Likewise, when you perform well, God is good. When you perform poorly...

God is good! Good is what God is, and your performance doesn't change Him.

> *You are good, and do good; teach me Your statutes.*
>
> (Psalm 119:68)

Anyone who is angry with God or is afraid of Him, either believes something wrong about Him or doesn't understand His character! There is never a reason for a believer to be afraid of Him or be mad at Him.

David was a man who understood this about God. He said in Psalm 34:8, *"Oh, taste and see that the Lord is good; blessed is the man who trusts in Him!"* Anyone who thinks God is anything but good didn't get a good taste!

Father, I believe You are good, and I am thankful for it! I believe I am secure because You have nothing but good for me!

Amen!

DAY 76

God Has Gifted Us

As each one has received a gift, minister it to one another, as good stewards of the manifold grace of God.

(1 Peter 4:10)

A very important truth is brought out in this verse from the use of the phrase "manifold grace of God." The Merriam-Webster Dictionary defines the word "manifold" as "marked by diversity or variety."[9] This means God's grace is multi-faceted. The Apostle Peter understood God's grace as having many different faces or elements to it, one of which is mentioned specifically in today's verse *"As each one has received a gift..."* Every one of us has been graced with a gift from God, a divine gratuity, a spiritual endowment.

This is a supernatural ability from God you didn't learn on your own or go to school to be taught. Don't ever think you don't have anything to offer or anything of worth to give or use! You have been given something from God, and He expects you to be a good steward of it! How do you do that? By being willing to "minister it to one another." The reason He gifted you is so you

---

9 "Manifold," Merriam-Webster Online Dictionary (Merriam-Webster, Incorporated, 2021), https://www.merriam-webster.com/dictionary/manifold.

can use the gift and be a blessing to others. You must discover what the gift is.

There are other faces of grace to mention. Ephesians 2:4 says, *"But God, who is rich in mercy, because of His great love with which He loved us."* **Mercy is that part of God's grace, which holds back what we deserve.** Boy, this is a great benefit we are enjoying from our God! None of us gets what we deserve; you should be thankful for that! Ephesians 2:7 tells us, *"that in the ages to come He might show the exceeding riches of His grace in His kindness toward us in Christ Jesus."* He has shown kindness to us through Jesus Christ! **Kindness is the part of God's grace that gives us what we do not deserve.**

God has a friendly disposition. His kindness extends His goodness and love to us at all times, even when we don't deserve it! *"And we have known and believed the love that God has for us. God is love..."* (1 John 4:16), (emphasis mine). Because **God is love** and **He is good**, His grace is evident toward us at all times. We should never think otherwise. We should have a constant awareness and expectancy of His love, goodness, mercy, and kindness as facets of His grace abounding toward us!

Father, I am so very thankful for the manifold grace of God. I believe Your grace is abundant toward me!
Amen!

DAY 77

God's Thoughts Toward You Are Peace and Not Evil

For I know the thoughts that I think toward you, says the Lord, thoughts of peace and not of evil, to give you a future and a hope.

(Jeremiah 29:11)

This has been a verse that has had much meaning to me for decades. The thoughts God thinks of us are *"thoughts of peace and not of evil."* If you have ever experienced low self-esteem or self-deprecating thoughts about yourself or your abilities, you can be confident God does not think that way of you. God loves you and believes in you, and thinks only good thoughts about you. He is for you and wants you to succeed in life.

This is brought out in the last phrase, *"to give you a future and a hope."* The context of Jeremiah, Chapter 29 is, the prophet sent a letter to people who were experiencing hardship in captivity. God promised them He had a plan for them in the midst of their current situation! If you have ever or are now facing challenges or a difficult situation, you can be comforted by this promise from God today. This is a promise that God has a plan for you regardless of your set of circumstances.

God is able to work in you and through you to prosper you and bring you along to the fulfillment of His plan for your life. You must understand it is necessary for you to cooperate with Him by faith. Some people have the idea if it is God's will, it will automatically come to pass. That is not correct. It is true God has a plan, and He desires good for you, but you must partner with Him in the process.

If you allow Him to, God will reveal His plan to you. This is brought out in the next two verses, *"Then you will call upon Me and go and pray to Me, and I will listen to you. And you will seek Me and find Me, when you search for Me with all your heart"* (Jeremiah 29:12–13). When you begin to sense God is directing you, it will take all of your strength and determination to begin to come into alignment with His will and purpose.

You will need a determined, committed faith which won't let go of God and His plan as you wait on Him to bring you out of your situation and into His plan,

But those who wait on the Lord shall renew their strength...
(Isaiah 40:31)

Father, I believe You have a plan to give me a future and a hope, and I receive it.
Amen!

DAY 78

We Are Partakers of the Divine Nature

Grace and peace be multiplied to you in the knowledge of God and of Jesus our Lord, as His divine power has given to us all things that pertain to life and godliness, through the knowledge of Him who called us by glory and virtue, by which have been given to us exceedingly great and precious promises, that through these you may be partakers of the divine nature, having escaped the corruption that is in the world through lust.

(2 Peter 1:2–4)

One of the great benefits we have as believers is "exceedingly great and precious promises" from our God have been given to us! These promises have been given for our benefit and are intended by God to be received by us and enjoyed. What a privilege it is to know God has given every believer all we need, which pertains to life and godliness! It's important to understand these promises are appropriated by faith,

"...through the knowledge of Him who called us by glory and virtue..."

(2 Peter 1:3)

Understand today; these promises have **already** been given to equip us to live a victorious Christian life! I just can't overstate the importance of everyone knowing what has been promised and what has been provided. Our faith is built as we know the promises in His Word (Romans 10:17). As much as we know, understand, and believe by faith, we are able to appropriate that which has been made available by His grace. God has enabled His divine power to be manifested in our lives.

The great promises God has made enable us to become "partakers of the divine nature" because we are one with Him. Colossians 1:26–27 tells us, *"the mystery which has been hidden from ages and from generations, but now has been revealed to His saints. To them God willed to make known what are the riches of the glory of this mystery among the Gentiles: which is Christ in you, the hope of glory."* This revealed mystery is Christ by the Holy Spirit, Who takes up permanent residence in every believer. As promised, Christ is formed in us through relationship, and the attributes of His nature begin to become evident in us!

The Apostle Paul clearly stated by the inspiration of the Holy Spirit, *"For all the promises of God in Him are Yes, and in Him Amen, to the glory of God through us"* (2 Corinthians 1:20). **God's response to all His promises to us in His Word is "yes"!** Your job is to believe!

Father God, I am thankful for every great and precious promise You have made!

Amen!

DAY 79

He Gives Comfort to Those Who Mourn

Blessed are those who mourn, for they shall be comforted.

(Matthew 5:4)

Jesus' Sermon on the Mount in Matthew, Chapter 5, begins with what we know as the "Beatitudes". The Beatitudes are "blessings" listed by Jesus. Today's verse communicates a great benefit available to all of us as believers; the blessing of comfort to all who mourn. For example, as a believer, you should be able to distinguish a great difference in the way you mourned the loss of a loved one before you were born again by receiving Jesus and the way you mourn after the new birth. **Our eternal perspective, formed by the unfailing promises we have from God, enables us to receive comfort from Him unknown to us prior.**

In addition to the promises we have from His Word, we also have the comforting presence of the Holy Spirit in our lives which was promised by Jesus. *"But when the Comforter is come, whom I will send unto you from the Father, even the Spirit of truth, which proceedeth from the Father, he shall testify of me"* (John 15:26

KJV). The Holy Spirit is God's gift to the Church. One of the major differences between the Old Testament saints and the New Testament saints is the indwelling presence of the Holy Spirit in the life of a Christian.

One of the ways the Holy Spirit helps us is, **He is our Comforter!** This important role of the precious Holy Spirit is mentioned in John 16:7 (KJV) as well, *"Nevertheless I tell you the truth; It is expedient for you that I go away: for if I go not away, the Comforter will not come unto you; but if I depart, I will send him unto you."* Jesus emphasized the necessity of His going away so it would be possible for the Holy Spirit to come to us.

It should be a great comfort to every believer to know the Holy Spirit now indwells us as believers to help, guide, and teach us (John 14:26). I want to encourage you to be aware of the great blessing it is to have this benefit available to us. Rely upon the Holy Spirit to guide you when you are facing difficult decisions. Rely upon Him to teach you and bring illumination and revelation from God. And know today we do not grieve and mourn as those who have no hope (1 Thessalonians 4:13)! We have an eternal perspective and hope the world does not have!

Father, I am thankful for the comforting presence of Your Spirit in my life. I rely upon You!
Amen!

DAY 80

The Lord Will Strengthen Our Heart

I would have lost heart, unless I had believed that I would see the goodness of the Lord in the land of the living. Wait on the Lord; be of good courage, and He shall strengthen your heart; wait, I say on the Lord!

(Psalm 27:13–14)

All of us have experienced delays or disappointments while waiting and hoping for something good to happen in our lives. The Bible says, *"Hope deferred, makes the heart sick..."* (Proverbs 13:12). It's not a fun thing to experience. No one wants it to happen, but when it does, how should we handle it?

First, I would say, at those times, remember delay is not denial. Don't automatically default to the worst scenario, assuming all is lost. I like to say, "the first report is not the last report." Don't lose faith because of a bad report or a delay. At those times, continue to believe you will see the goodness of the Lord! He's for you, and know His faithfulness is unfailing!

Next, notice it says to *"...wait on the Lord."* Most of the time, when we hear the word "wait," we tend to define it as to "remain in anticipation of something to happen," as in patiently holding on. But it also has another meaning, as in waiting on a table. This is the meaning which applies here. A good waiter at your favorite restaurant is attentive; he's observant of your needs. He's quick to "wait" on you to refill your glass before it is empty and pays attention to you to ensure you are well served.

We are being encouraged by the psalmist to "wait" on the Lord in much the same way. In those times, draw near to Him, attend to Him, know He is with you, and for you. **Minister to God through praise and thanksgiving. Replace frustration, discouragement, and depression by praising your way to victory.** As you do, you will discover He will strengthen your heart. Joy, peace, and faith will return, enabling you to believe from your heart to receive from Him!

Father God, help me to wait on You, to worship You and serve You as You deserve. Help me to trust I will see Your goodness in my life.

Amen!

DAY 81

God is Faithful to His Covenant with Us

Nevertheless My lovingkindness I will not utterly take from him, nor allow My faithfulness to fail. My covenant I will not break, nor alter the word that has gone out of My lips.

(Psalm 89:33–34)

It should be understood by all that God's character is faultless! "Faithfulness" can be defined in a number of different ways. To be faithful is to be constant in the performance of one's duties, to be true to one's word, or one who is trustworthy and reliable. It could also mean one who is steadfast in affection, allegiance, and loyalty. God's faithfulness is all of these things! His loyalty to us and His integrity is unfailing!

The psalmist knew this well. It should be well known by us too. Hebrews 13:5 tells us, *"Let your conduct be without covetousness; be content with such things as you have. For He Himself has said, 'I will never leave you nor forsake you.'"* God has promised never to leave or forsake us. This means He will not abandon us. As our Father, He can be trusted to meet all of our needs. He desires to be the source of all your supply.

Today's verse tells us, *"My covenant I will not break, nor alter the word that has gone out of My lips."* Our God is a covenant-making, promise-keeping God. This guarantees us He will keep His Word. So often in today's culture, we find people who are unfaithful or won't keep their word, but this is not so with our Father.

> *"God is not a man, that He should lie, nor a son of man, that He should repent. Has He said, and will He not do? Or has He spoken, and will He not make it good?"*
>
> (Numbers 23:19)

What do you need from God today? Find a verse or several which address your need, and believe them. With the understanding of God's faithfulness I am describing today, ask God to meet that need based upon what He has promised. Your faith will come alive as you hear the Word (Romans 10:17), then choose to believe and speak (2 Corinthians 4:13) the promise from Him. The reason many operate in doubt is they don't really believe God will not allow His faithfulness to fail. They doubt His loyalty to them because they have failed Him in some way. God's character is based totally upon His love and goodness, not yours.

Father God, I believe in Your faithfulness and integrity. I want You to know I trust You as my provider.
Amen!

DAY 82

We Have a Promise of Resurrection

For if we believe that Jesus died and rose again, even so God will bring with Him those who sleep in Jesus.

(1 Thessalonians 4:14)

All who have placed faith in Christ as their Savior have the assurance of being resurrected to new life from the dead. The Apostle Paul is the author of today's verse; his perspective is clear; the resurrection of Jesus assures us we too will be resurrected! Jesus led the way in resurrection for all of His people to follow. Those of us who have received Jesus by placing faith in Him will experience the promised resurrection. Jesus said,

"A little while longer and the world will see Me no more, but you will see Me. Because I live, you will live also."

(John 14:19)

First Corinthians, Chapter 15, makes the most complete doctrinal statement on the subject of the resurrection in all of Scripture. The Apostle Paul's revelation on this subject is invaluable to us. *"For as in Adam all die, even so in Christ all shall be made alive*" (1 Corinthians 15:22). Death, as a result of Adam's fall, comes to everyone. There are no exceptions. Likewise, our bodily resurrection will happen to everyone. Whether they believe in it or not, the resurrection of every person who has ever lived will happen. An eternal existence in either heaven or hell will become a reality.

> *Therefore let that abide in you which you heard from the beginning. If what you heard from the beginning abides in you, you also will abide in the Son and in the Father. And this is the promise that He has promised us—eternal life.*
>
> (1 John 2:24–25)

The Apostle John, under the inspiration of the Holy Spirit, described our eternal existence as "life". Jesus defined eternal life for us in John 17:3, "*And this is eternal life, that they may know You, the only true God, and Jesus Christ whom You have sent.*" Eternal life is not just existing forever. Eternal life is **knowing** "*the only true God, and Jesus Christ whom You have sent,*" so we may enjoy life with Him in heaven.

It is important for you to understand that death never means cessation of existence. For us as believers, the resurrection will enable us to enjoy eternal life in the presence of our Father forever. This is an awesome benefit we have from our God, which, if understood, will remove fear because death has no sting for us as believers (1 Corinthians 15:55)!

Heavenly Father, I believe in the resurrection, and I'm thankful death has lost its sting!

Amen!

DAY 83

Dying Grace at Life's End

But he, being full of the Holy Spirit, gazed into heaven and saw the glory of God, and Jesus standing at the right hand of God, and said, "Look! I see the heavens opened and the Son of Man standing at the right hand of God!"

(Acts 7:55–56)

This is an amazing story recorded for us in the Book of Acts, Chapter 7, about the martyrdom of Stephen. Stephen was the first martyr of the Church. His name first appears in Chapter 6 as he was selected by the early Church to be one of the first appointed deacons. Even though Stephen was not named as a preacher, pastor, or evangelist, Acts 6:8 tells us,

And Stephen, full of faith and power, did great wonders and signs among the people.

As a result, various sects of the religious Jews came against him with false accusations. Having been brought up on these false charges, Stephen was allowed to give his defense, which is recorded in Acts, Chapter 7. His defense is actually an amazing teaching from the Old Testament, He pointed out to them, just as their predecessors resisted the Holy Spirit, they likewise were resisting the Holy Spirit. Verse 54 tells us,

> *When they heard these things they were cut to the heart, and they gnashed at him with their teeth.*

When his accusers could no longer stand the conviction, they began to attack him, and an amazing thing happened. An anointing from God came upon him, and he saw into heaven where Jesus was *"standing at the right hand of God!"* As though Jesus was standing to honor His servant at his martyrdom! As Stephen's life was being taken from him, God anointed him with a **dying grace!**

At times people wonder, "How will I handle death?" Often, we hear testimonies from people at death's door. They speak of seeing angels or a bright light. It seems God allows a person for a moment to experience both realms as they are welcomed into heaven. This is dying grace! When we approach death, God is not far from us. No, God is near! *"Precious in the sight of the Lord is the death of His saints"* (Psalm 116:15). As death draws near to a believer, we can be confident God is with us and extends His grace to provide peace and assurance as we pass from this life to the next.

Father, it comforts me to know You are with me and will always be! I believe Your grace is abundant to help me at all times!
Amen!

DAY 84

We Have Peace with God

Therefore, having been justified by faith, we have peace with God through our Lord Jesus Christ.

(Romans 5:1)

Peace is the birthright of every believer! There are two types to be understood: peace **with** God and the peace **of** God. Peace with God means we have been declared innocent. Therefore, there is no fear of punishment for the things we did which were deserving of punishment. The punishment we deserved was placed on Jesus as our substitute. As a result, justification is the announcement that the sinner is not guilty. The war between God and man was ended by Jesus' accomplishment at the cross, and now peace has come!

We must have a working knowledge of the truth of our justification before God to live the victorious Christian life. It is impossible to imagine any believer experiencing total victory in their life without peace. This verse tells us peace **with** God comes to us as a result of being justified by faith.

The layman's definition of justified is: It's just-as-if-I'd never sinned! The first thing God does for the sinner at the new birth is to render him/her just or innocent in His sight! This is an instantaneous event. It's not earned by our performance or good works. It is freely given and received by faith as a benefit of our salvation and is intended by God to be enjoyed by His children.

Peace with God means there is no reason to struggle with a sense of guilt from the sins of our past. There is no need to carry excessive remorse for the mistakes and bad choices made in life before our new birth.

The peace **of** God is a sense that everything is going to be alright! Our Father desires and has promised to sustain us (Psalm 55:22) and care for us in every way. Philippians 4:6–7 tells us, *"Be anxious for nothing, but in everything by prayer and supplication, with thanksgiving, let your requests be made known to God; and the peace of God, which surpasses all understanding, will guard your hearts and minds through Christ Jesus."* As we make our requests known to God, there should be an accompanying peace guarding our heart and mind. It brings a sense that we are safe in the hands of our God!

Heavenly Father, thank you for peace, for justifying me by faith in my Lord Jesus, and thank you for the assurance I have in You.

In Jesus' name...

Amen!

DAY 85

We Have Been Accepted in the Beloved

To the praise of the glory of His grace, by which He made us accepted in the beloved.

(Ephesians 1:6)

This is a statement of praise from the Apostle Paul for the grace of God. God deals with us strictly by grace. **It is through the grace of God that we have been accepted.** It is not due to any effort of our own that God accepts us. This is so important to understand. Most people have a "performance mentality" when it comes to pleasing God. They tend to think, *Do good, get good.* In other words, people tend to think they get what they deserve from God. Therefore, they have the idea the only way to be accepted is to earn it by being good or doing good.

Paul is making the point here, praise God, it is only by the grace of God which causes us to be accepted by Him! Grace is unearned and undeserved favor. **Any attempt to earn acceptance makes grace of no effect.** The only way for us to please God is to approach Him humbly by faith. *"But without faith it is impossible to please Him, for he who comes to God must believe that He* *is, and that He is a rewarder of those who diligently seek Him"* (Hebrews 11:6). When God sees our faith, it pleases Him.

Even if we have fallen short and failed to attain a perceived standard of holiness or performance, God accepts us because of our faith in Him. I hope you are grasping the value of this great benefit we have in serving our God. Imagine never being able to perform well enough to be accepted by Him. Every time you approached Him, you would feel guilty and unworthy. His grace has eliminated all of that.

The word "accept" is defined by the *Merriam-Webster Dictionary* as "to receive willingly; to agree to."[10] Having been "accepted in the beloved" means God has agreed to willingly receive us as we are! God does not just tolerate us; He actually loves us and likes us! Zephaniah 3:17 says, *"The Lord your God in your midst, the Mighty One, will save; He will rejoice over you with gladness, He will quiet you with His love, He will rejoice over you with singing."* God's love for you is extravagant. If you are understanding His acceptance as I am describing, it will enable you to enjoy a peaceful relationship with God.

Father God, thank you for acceptance! By faith, I believe Your grace is abundant, and I am accepted in the beloved!
Amen!

---

10 Accept," Merriam-Webster Online Dictionary (Merriam-Webster, Incorporated, 2021), https://www.merriam-webster.com/dictionary/accept.

DAY 86

We Have a Promise of Provision

"Therefore I say to you, do not worry about your life, what
you will eat or what you will drink; nor about your body,
what you will put on. Is not life more than food and the body
more than clothing?"

(Matthew 6:25)

At an early age (too young), I was married with children and had the responsibility of raising a family as the primary breadwinner. Being unskilled and untrained in any vocation, I was working as a laborer in the construction trade. I was able to earn enough money in my work when I was able to work steady but was often laid off in the wintertime or at the end of the job. Complicating it further, I had incurred too much debt as a result of my lack of financial discipline, not to mention the challenge of meeting the needs of my family.

I was working in the northwest corner of Colorado in the early 80s before I had made my decision to turn my life around to live for God. Winter was approaching, and I was missing some work due to weather conditions, which was really complicating my financial situation. I was sitting at home one day, unable to work, worrying about money. I was a world-class worrier! I picked up a Bible and found these verses in Matthew, Chapter 6. Jesus taught in these verses about God's desire and ability to supply our needs, food, shelter, and clothing (Matthew 6:26–31).

For the first time in my life, I was being ministered to by the Word of God. I sensed the Lord dealing with me as the words pierced my heart. The Bible came powerfully alive to me at that moment. It was something God used at a time when He was drawing me by His Spirit. It was only a few months later, as a result of being witnessed to by a friend at work and opening my heart to God, I made the decision to turn my life around. I received Jesus as Lord and was genuinely born again!

One of the greatest things I have learned is, *"Now if God so clothes the grass of the field, which today is, and tomorrow is thrown into the oven, will He not much more clothe you, O you of little faith?"* (Matthew 6:30). It's a great benefit we have in enjoying a relationship with our God! We just have to learn to cooperate with Him by placing faith in Him rather than in our own abilities!

Lord God, as my Father, I know You will provide for me. I thank you today!

Amen!

DAY 87

God's Word Illuminates Our Path

Your word is a lamp to my feet and a light to my path.

(Psalm 119:105)

Have you ever had an accident attempting to walk in the dark? Boy, I have! I remember a time many years ago, I got out of bed in the night, and not wanting to disturb my wife, I was carefully making my way out of the bedroom in total darkness. Having bumped into things in the dark before, I was carefully moving toward the door of the bedroom with my arms stretched out in front of me, "feeling" my way. I thought the door was open wide and was attempting to move through the opening. The door was halfway ajar, and it managed to slip between my arms in the dark when suddenly I walked directly into the edge of the open door! It struck me solidly right on my nose and mouth! Ouch! We now use night lights.

Just as it is dangerous to attempt to walk in the darkness, it can be dangerous to attempt to make decisions without the illuminating effect of the Word of God! Our God has promised His Word will be a lamp to our feet and a light to our path. All of our decisions should be made by considering the counsel of God's Word. We are instructed by Ephesians 5:8, *"For you were once darkness, but now you are light in the Lord. Walk as children of light."* This verse emphasizes the point that we *"are light in the Lord."* A true believer becomes light (which includes all the goodness of God) the moment he/she is born again. It is the nature of a Christian to walk in the light rather than walking in darkness.

When we were lost, we were children of darkness or the devil. As Christians, we are full-time children of the light. It's who we are. It's our nature. It needs to become our experience. It is not okay for us to walk in darkness. Our lives are to be directed and regulated by God's Word lighting our path. This means the Bible is to be the guiding standard in our lives. The daily choices we make should be influenced by what God has told us. The Bible is a practical guide we use to give us the confidence to do the right thing! It's a great benefit God has given to help us navigate life!

Father, please give me understanding from Your Word to help me make right choices as I walk in the light and not in darkness!
Amen!

DAY 88

The Word is Life and Health to Our Flesh

My son, give attention to my words; incline your ear to my sayings. Do not let them depart from your eyes; keep them in the midst of your heart; for they are life to those who find them, and health to all their flesh.

(Proverbs 4:20–22)

These verses speak to us of the value of the Word of God in our life. We are to give attention to God's words, to incline our ear to His sayings, to keep them in the midst of our heart. When we value the Word of God in this way, we have a promise from Him; they (God's words) *"...are life to those who find them, and health to all their flesh."*

The word "health" in verse 22 is translated from the Hebrew word "marpe," which is defined as "remedy, cure, or medicine."[11] It could actually be used this way and do no damage to the text, *"for they are life to those who find them, and health* (medicine) *to all their flesh"* (emphasis mine). I have come to understand and love this great benefit our God has made available to us! Un-

11 "Strong's Hebrew: 4832" (Bible Hub, 2021), https://biblehub.com/he-brew/4832.htm.

189

fortunately, many people don't understand this. We can use the Word of God as a preventative "medicine" to our flesh. Often, people who believe in divine healing never try to access it until they become sick or start to show symptoms. Then they will pray to God, or if they are a "faith person," they will begin to quote or confess the Scripture.

I am thankful God is our healer, and healing is part of the atonement provided us, but can I say to you, **divine health is better than divine healing!** Healing is awesome, but it is better not to need to be healed! If you will believe and begin to use your faith (believing and speaking) for divine health, you can apply God's Word in this way to receive *"health to all their flesh."* The Apostle John made a great statement in 3 John 1:2, *"Beloved, I pray that you may prosper in all things and be in health, just as your soul prospers."* God desires for us to prosper and be in health, but notice, it is qualified. We will prosper and be in health according to the degree we prosper our soul! It matters what you believe about this, which is why we...

> *Study to shew thyself approved unto God, a workman that needeth not to be ashamed, rightly dividing the word of truth.*
>
> (2 Timothy 2:15 KJV)

Heavenly Father, I believe Your powerful Word is working in me to provide health to my flesh!
Amen!

DAY 89

Our Provision is a Byproduct of Seeking God First

But seek first the kingdom of God and His righteousness,
and all these things shall be added to you.

(Matthew 6:33)

Today's verse is part of the Sermon on the Mount Jesus preached in Matthew, Chapters 5 through 7. It is a powerful sermon Jesus delivered to His disciples, training His ministry team. This portion of the sermon emphasizes reliance upon God for the provision of all our needs. God desires to be the source of all our supply, and this is the reason Jesus makes the point in today's verse that we should seek first the kingdom of God and His righteousness. Because it is so easy to lust after money and the things it can provide, God has provided a system where prosperity is a byproduct of putting God first in our lives.

There is no shortage in the kingdom of God. We need to exchange our poverty mindset for a provision mindset. As long as our priority is seeking first the kingdom of God and taking care of His business, He will provide everything we need. Jesus said in Matthew 6:25, *"Therefore I say to you, do not worry about your life, what you will eat or what you will drink; nor about your body, what you will put on. Is not life more than food and the body more than clothing?"* When you are focused upon your relationship with your God and King, seeking Him and His kingdom business, there will be no need to worry about the provision of daily necessities. You will find God can and will take better care of you than you can take care of yourself!

This is one of the greatest benefits of living for God I have found in my life. It has taken a renewing of my mind (Romans 12:2) in order to view life totally from this perspective. Money is not evil, it is a necessary part of life, but it is not to be our highest priority. **God is not against money. He is against us serving money,** *"No one can serve two masters; for either he will hate the one and love the other, or else he will be loyal to the one and despise the other. You cannot serve God and mammon"* (Matthew 6:24). You can have God and riches, but you must serve only one of them. No matter what our situation, we can focus on the kingdom and say with confidence, "My God will supply!"

Father, I am comforted and confident knowing You can and will provide for me as I seek first Your Kingdom and righteousness!
Amen!

DAY 90

A Stable Christian Life

Wisdom and knowledge will be the stability of your times, and the strength of salvation; the fear of the Lord is His treasure.

(Isaiah 33:6)

Today's verse is relatively obscure. I rarely hear it referenced by ministers, yet it contains a powerful truth I consider to be a great benefit of walking with our God. If you can understand the truth being communicated in this verse, it will greatly help you to experience a stable Christian life. I have learned it is possible to have stability in our walk with the Lord. I have known Christians who have a "yo-yo" type of existence. What I mean is, one time you see them, they are excited and on a mountaintop spiritually. The next time you see them, they are in a valley. There is no stability in their walk with the Lord; they vacillate from excitement to depression.

Life doesn't have to be a roller-coaster existence like this. Today's verse is giving us keys to experiencing the stability we all need. It says, *"Wisdom and knowledge will be the stability of your times."* Knowledge is an input; wisdom is an output. When we correctly apply knowledge, it comes out in the form of wisdom.

It is our responsibility to gain knowledge of God's Word and then apply it correctly in our lives in the form of wisdom. When done correctly, the result is stability in our life.

Jesus taught this principle in Matthew 7:24–25, *"Therefore whoever hears these sayings of Mine, and does them, I will liken him to a wise man who built his house on the rock: and the rain descended, the floods came, and the winds blew and beat on that house; and it did not fall, for it was founded on the rock."* When you hear the Word and do the Word, you are like a wise man whose house is built on a rock. When the storms of life come, they don't crash your house in! Storms come to everyone's life, but it is possible to be stable even in the midst of a storm!

Living by faith does not mean storms won't come, but living by faith means we can overcome them all! In consistency lies the power. In order for Bible truth to produce lasting fruit in your life, you will need to apply it consistently! Make the commitment to learn God's Word and do it. Expect to be an overcomer (1 John 5:4; Romans 8:37).

Father, I believe as I apply Your Word in my life, I can experience stability with You!

Amen!

DAY 91

Jesus is Enough for You

...Have I been with you so long and yet you have not known me, Philip? He who has seen Me has seen the Father; so how can you say, "Show us the Father"?

(John 14:9)

Recently, at the Kyle Correctional Center, where I am Chaplain, I was approached by a man who said he wanted to speak with me. When I asked him what it was about, he told me he had decided he wanted to convert to Christianity. I said, "Awesome!" I then asked, "Do you believe God sent Jesus for us? To which he replied, "Yes." I then asked, "Do you believe Jesus died for your sins?" He then told me he was having a hard time believing one man could do that.

It reminds me of Philip's comment to Jesus from John 14:8, *"Lord, show us the Father, and it is sufficient for us."* In other words, Jesus, you are not enough but, if You will reveal God to us, that will be enough. Although Philip had seen Jesus and had been with Him, he still didn't realize Jesus is God! Jesus' response to him is quoted above.

When Jesus died on the cross for us, it wasn't just a man giving His life. Jesus was God in the flesh. His life was worth more than every human life which could ever exist. When Jesus shed His blood for us, it was worth much more than all of humanity. One drop of Jesus' blood was sufficient to wash away our sin, redeem us to God and purchase our life and salvation! If you can envision a balance scale with Jesus' blood on one side and all of humanity on the other, it would tip entirely to the side of the blood of Jesus.

His life blood is infinitely more valuable than our lives and sufficient to pay the penalty to satisfy God's claim of justice! One of the strongest arguments for the deity of Jesus in all of Scripture is found in John 5:23,

> *that all should honor the Son just as they honor the Father. He who does not honor the Son does not honor the Father who sent Him.*

It isn't enough to honor Jesus. We have to honor Him just as we honor the Father. Know this, Jesus is enough for you! In Him, you will find everything you could ever need!

Father, thank you for what Jesus has done for me! I believe His death has made it possible to have relationship with You.
Amen!

DAY 92

The Name of Jesus is a
Tower of Safety

The name of the Lord is a strong tower; the righteous run to it and are safe.

(Proverbs 18:10)

In my conversations with people, I am hearing a lot of confusion about God's protection of His people. For example, in the prison facility, I hear mixed ideas. Most of it is associated with a performance mentality. When I speak of my faith in God for protection, they will often say something which makes me know they believe God will protect me because I am a preacher, but maybe the same protection isn't available for them.

They have the idea God is a respecter of persons and will provide protection if we have earned it or deserve it because of our good works, which isn't true at all. God's power doesn't work for us because we are so deserving. It is available for every Christian if they will believe for it.

One of my favorite verses is Proverbs 18:10, *"The name of the Lord is a strong tower; the righteous run to it and are safe."* It doesn't say the preachers run to it or the most deserving. It says the "righteous" run to it and find safety. This is a promise for every born-again believer. **Every person who has received Jesus is the righteous** (2 Corinthians 5:21). The strong name of Jesus provides protection for us.

Notice Philippians 2:9–11,

> "Therefore God also has highly exalted Him and given Him the name which is above every name, that at the name of Jesus every knee should bow, of those in heaven, and of those on earth, and of those under the earth, and that every tongue should confess that Jesus Christ is Lord, to the glory of God the Father."

The name of Jesus has authority in three realms, heaven, earth, and under the earth.

When we use the name of Jesus in faith, we should expect power to accompany the name. The name of Jesus is above every name! Most Christians believe God has power, but few believe it is for us and toward us on our behalf. Our right to use the name of Jesus provides a tower of safety for us. One of the greatest joys I have in relationship with my God is to know I am safe in the hands of God!

Heavenly Father, I believe the name of Jesus is powerful and provides a tower of safety for me!
Amen!

DAY 93

God Cares for Us Affectionately and Watchfully

Casting all your care upon Him, for He cares for you.

(1 Peter 5:7)

The goal of a good cast when you are fishing at the lake is to throw the bait as far away from you as possible into the water. It requires some hand and eye coordination to release at the correct moment, so the bait does not drop behind you or slam down in front of you. When you reach back and throw forward and release at the top of the arc, you have made a good cast, and the bait leaves you and drops far into the lake!

The same objective applies when we are casting all of our care on the Lord! We are commanded in today's verse to cast all of our care, all of our anxieties, all our worries, all our concerns on Him. Easy to say, sometimes not so easy to do! The reason this is difficult is that our cares are too important to us; they are precious to us. We have the tendency to hold tight in order to attend to them ourselves. In order to do this correctly, there is something you must believe and know well;

He cares for you affectionately and cares about you watchfully.

(1 Peter 5:7 AMP)

Once you believe God can and will take better care of that which concerns you than you can do yourself, you will be able to cast your cares on Him! Rather than holding on to our cares, worries, and concerns, we are to cast them on Him then replace them with *"whatever things are true, whatever things are noble, whatever things are just, whatever things are pure, whatever things are lovely, whatever things are of good report, if there is any virtue and if there is anything praiseworthy—meditate on these things"* (Philippians 4:8). I am describing for you one of the great benefits we have from God, which will produce a peaceful life.

This is communicated for us beautifully in Isaiah 26:3, *"You will keep him in perfect peace, whose mind is stayed on You, because he trusts in You."* The word "peace" is translated from the Hebrew word "shalom," which is defined as well, happy, health, prosperity, or safety.[12] When we choose to keep our mind stayed on Him, the result is peace in our life. When we choose to meditate on our cares and worries, the result is depression, fear, or anxiety. Cast your care upon Him and be at peace!

Father, I choose to cast all my care on You. I know today You care for me!

Amen!

---

12 "H7965 - Šālôm - Strong's Hebrew Lexicon (KJV)," Strong's Hebrew Lexicon (KJV) (Blueletterbible, 2021), https://www.blueletterbible.org/lang/lexicon/lexicon.cfm?t=kjv&strongs=h7965.

DAY 94

God is Our Refuge and Fortress

He who dwells in the secret place of the Most High shall abide under the shadow of the Almighty. I will say of the Lord, "He is my refuge and my fortress; my God, in Him I will trust.

(Psalm 91:1–2)

The 91st Psalm is a beautiful psalm of protection and deliverance. Notice, this is a promise of protection for those who dwell in the secret place of the Most High. This is for those who dwell there, not just wish and hope, or visit occasionally! Those who dwell in the secret place of the Most High are the ones who abide in Christ (John 15:4). Abiding in Christ gives us entrance into the protection of the shadow of the Almighty!

Notice verse 2 says, *"I will say of the Lord, 'He is my refuge and my fortress; my God, in Him I will trust.'"* Many Christians mistakenly think this is automatic for them simply because they are believers. This verse clearly says, *"I will **say** of the Lord..."* It is important to understand we have a part to play in experiencing the protection and deliverance being spoken of in this verse!

The promises of God are voice activated. **Our words, when spoken in faith, release and activate the power of God in our life.** Often Christians who don't understand this approach God in prayer as beggars pleading with Him to protect without any cooperation of their own. The way we cooperate in this process is by believing and speaking to activate the power!

We can actually set *"...on fire the course of nature..."* (James 3:6) with our tongue. James employed this principle in a negative sense, emphasizing it is set on fire by hell. But Proverbs 18:21 tells us, *"Death and life are in the power of the tongue..."* When you speak the promises of God, you release life and protection, but when you speak fear or doubt, you release death, thus setting on fire the course of nature! When we *"...say of the Lord, 'He is my refuge and my fortress...'"* we enter into the place of His safety and protection. We can employ the use of the strong name of Jesus as well, Proverbs 18:10,

> *The name of the Lord is a strong tower; the righteous run to it and are safe.*

This is promising supernatural protection that many Christians don't believe is possible. They are correct. If they don't believe it enough to say it, it won't be possible for them to receive it! You must believe to receive it, and say it to activate it!

Heavenly Father, I say You are my refuge and my fortress!
I receive my protection in Jesus' strong name...
Amen!

DAY 95

God Will Complete the Good Work in Us

being confident of this very thing, that He who has begun a good work in you will complete it until the day of Jesus Christ;

(Philippians 1:6)

Our salvation is an ongoing experience. We aren't supposed to put our faith in Jesus to be born again and then never think about it again. Receiving Jesus to be born again and forgiven of our sins is a necessary step to receiving our eternal salvation, but the new birth is merely the first step, not the end! In today's verse, the Apostle Paul expressed confidence that the good work he started in the Philippians, the Lord would continue and complete. You should have the same expectation about your life.

God desires to complete a good work in all of our lives, but it is not automatic; we have to cooperate with Him to enable Him to accomplish what He wants to do in us! We make mistakes and fail at times, and **our faithfulness may be suspect, but God's faithfulness never is!** It is always His will to complete the good work in us. I may not be what I am supposed to be, but thank God I am not what I used to be! You can probably say the same. We are all in process *"For a righteous man may fall seven times and rise again, but the wicked shall fall by calamity"* (Proverbs 24:16). When you fall, get up! If you fall seven times, keep getting up. Don't run away from God; run to Him.

Paul the Apostle was arguably the greatest Christian to have ever lived, but he described this process of maturity in Philippians 3:12, *"Not as though I had already attained, either were already perfect: but I follow after, if that I may apprehend that for which also I am apprehended of Christ Jesus"* (KJV). The word "perfect" is used in Scripture to describe spiritual maturity. Paul was certainly mature spiritually when he wrote this, but he was not flawless or without defect yet. Even he was in process.

There is a perseverance, which is necessary for the Christian life. Paul was expressing confidence in God's ability to bring us along to *"...apprehend that for which also I am apprehended of Christ Jesus."* God does not see you as a failure. He sees you as a learner. He's not heaping condemnation on you for your mistakes; His lovingkindness is abundant, and He desires to work with you to complete the good work He has begun in you!

Father, I am thankful today that You are working in me to complete Your good work!
Amen!

DAY 96

There is No Need to Be Afraid or Dismayed

"Have I not commanded you? Be strong and of good courage; do not be afraid, nor be dismayed, for the Lord your God is with you wherever you go."

(Joshua 1:9)

In Joshua, Chapter 1, we are told Joshua was chosen by God and faced the daunting task of replacing Moses as the leader of Israel. The phrase *"Be strong and of good courage"* is repeated four times in this chapter and is God's encouragement to Joshua intended to help him to accomplish the great task God had called him to. Moses was a seasoned leader. Joshua was relatively untried. I can imagine he was feeling insecure or afraid, thus the reason God told him,

"...Be strong and of good courage; do not be afraid, nor be dismayed, for the Lord your God is with you wherever you go."

The word "dismayed" is defined as "to cause to lose courage, or to dishearten."[13] Joshua probably felt the weight of the responsibility which had shifted upon him as God's chosen leader. God encouraged him to believe God was with him. Have you ever felt dismayed in your walk with the Lord? I have. Reminding ourselves of this same truth will encourage and strengthen us as well. I have used Psalm 27:13–14 to encourage myself when I felt dismayed, *"I would have lost heart, unless I had believed that I would see the goodness of the Lord in the land of the living. Wait on the Lord; be of good courage, and He shall strengthen your heart; wait, I say, on the Lord!"* The hope of God's loyalty and faithfulness to us will keep us from losing heart. David said he **believed** he would see the goodness of the Lord in the land of the living!

It really matters what you believe when you begin to feel afraid or dismayed. Refuse to receive the thoughts (2 Corinthians 10:3–5) which bombard your mind and choose to believe God is with you and expect to see the goodness of the Lord on your behalf! It is important to take your eyes off of that which is threatening you and causing fear and, as an act of your will, make a choice to *"...walk by faith and not by sight"* (2 Corinthians 5:7). You have the unfailing promise of the faithfulness of God. You have every reason to believe God is with you and will help you by sustaining you through it all (Psalm 55:22). Do not be afraid or dismayed!

Father God, I believe You are with me wherever I go. I will not be afraid or dismayed in the name of Jesus!

Amen!

---

13 "Dismay," In *Merriam-Webster Online Dictionary* (Merriam-Webster, Incorporated, 2012), https://www.merriam-webster.com/dictionary/dismay.

DAY 97

We Have Received the Mind of Christ

For "who has known the mind of the Lord that he may instruct Him?" But we have the mind of Christ.

(1 Corinthians 2:16)

Some years back, there was a Christian man incarcerated at the Kyle Correctional Center who was a talented guitar player. He became involved in our Chapel services with me and began to help with the praise and worship team at church. I encourage the men in my preaching to memorize Scripture verses as an important spiritual discipline. Talking to him about it, he said, "Chaplain, my drug addiction has damaged my memory, and I can't memorize verses." I explained to him that he was able to remember song lyrics from many years ago, and if he wanted to memorize Scripture as well, he could with the help of the Holy Spirit. He understood and said, "You are right!" He was failing to consider God's help in this.

The Apostle Paul made quite a statement in today's verse! He didn't say we have a portion of the wisdom of Christ transferred to us; he said, "*...we have the mind of Christ*"! It is obvious to us our natural mind doesn't know everything. Our physical brain is limited and does not know all things. This is referenced in the previous verses, *"But the natural man does not receive the things of the Spirit of God, for they are foolishness to him; nor can he know them, because they are spiritually discerned"* (1 Corinthians 2:14). At the new birth, it is our spirit that becomes the new creation and is alive unto God (2 Corinthians 5:17).

As a Christian, one-third of our salvation is complete (Colossians 2:10). It is the spirit of a born-again man who is *"... renewed in knowledge according the image of Him who created him"* (Colossians 3:10). Our born-again spirit contains the mind of Christ; our physical brain does not. This is why renewing our physical mind is so important! (Romans 12:2). The rest of the Christian life is a process of renewing the mind and releasing what is in our spirit. In this way, our spirit man will feed us information through our soul (mind, will, emotions), helping us to access the wisdom of the mind of Christ. Understanding this will benefit you greatly in your daily life, applying the wisdom of God received from the mind of Christ. I encourage you not to fail to consider what the Lord has done in you to help you in this area.

Father, thank you for giving me the mind of Christ to help me with wisdom from You!
Amen!

DAY 98

God Provides All Sufficiency for Every Good Work

And God is able to make all grace abound toward you, that you, always having all sufficiency in all things, may have an abundance for every good work.

(2 Corinthians 9:8)

The Book of 2 Corinthians, Chapters 8 and 9, deal with money and instructions about the importance of giving to God. Paul the Apostle deals with Christ's example as well as our motivation for giving. Then in today's verse, he makes the point, "... *God is able to make all grace abound...*" Notice he did not say, "God will make all grace abound toward you." God is willing and able to supply every need of a cheerful giver, but it does not happen automatically. As I have pointed out many times, we have to cooperate with Him in His ways.

There are things we do to activate the supply, such as; giving cheerfully (2 Corinthians 9:7), giving with the right motive (1 Corinthians 13:3), and not growing weary while doing good

(Galatians 6:9). When our giving is mixed with faith, as well as these important traits, we can expect to reap abundantly!

Notice it is God's desire for His people to *"...have an abundance for every good work."* His desire is to do more than simply meet your bare necessities; He desires for us to have all sufficiency in all things! He is able to make all grace abound toward us, so we are abundantly supplied, then we can be generous with others. The purpose of prosperity is not just so we are able to build wealth to consume it upon our lusts. The purpose of prosperity is that we are able to have our needs abundantly supplied, then be able to give to every good work. God desires for us to be able to be a blessing to others who are in need and be able to fund or contribute to every good work.

I'm describing a great benefit we have with God. Unfortunately, there are religious people who actually teach against this and others who simply do not know. Hosea 4:6 says, *"My people are destroyed for lack of knowledge..."* **God's people are being destroyed and living below their rights and privileges because of a lack of knowledge of these things.** People say, "What you don't know won't hurt you." Not true! What you don't know is killing you! Remember, God wants us to prosper and be in health as our soul prospers (3 John 1:2).

Father, I am thankful to know You want me to have an abundance, so I am able to give to every good work!
Amen!

DAY 99

We Are Sanctified in Christ Jesus

To the church of God which is at Corinth, to those who are sanctified in Christ Jesus, called to be saints, with all who in every place call on the name of Jesus Christ our Lord, both theirs and ours.

(1 Corinthians 1:2)

Recently while driving past a local church, I noticed their marquee sign which read, "God saw you do that!" I pondered their message to the community; to me, it communicated, "God is gonna get you." There are a lot of people who think this way about God. Because of their law-based, performance mentality they picture God in their mind as a judgmental, condemning God out to get His people when they sin. Today's verse gives us some insight to counter the incorrect view many hold, which is often promoted by some churches and ministers.

Notice again what he said, *"To the church of God which is at Corinth, to those who are sanctified in Christ Jesus, called to be saints..."* He addressed his letter to the "church in Corinth... the saints in Corinth". This is significant, and there is a great lesson to be understood.

This is the same group of people he is correcting in this epistle! There were a variety of issues within the church. Paul was writing to address things such as incest, conduct in their services, abuse of the spiritual gifts, and bad doctrine, just to name a few. He greeted these believers as sanctified in Christ! **This verse makes it clear our sanctification is a gift obtained through salvation by faith... not something we earn.** Every believer in Christ is sanctified. We do not earn this distinction with our good performance, nor do we lose it through our poor performance! This is the essence of God's grace.

Someone may ask, "Are you saying it is okay to sin?" No! There is a valid reason not to sin. Sin opens the door to the devil, which allows him to kill, steal, and destroy (John 10:10). Sin affects your relationship with the devil, but it does not affect your relationship with God! Even though those believers had problems, God still viewed them as sanctified believers! And this is the way He views you and me as believers as well. Understanding this will correct a lot of errors in the way people view their relationship with God. God is not out to get you. He desires to have a beautiful relationship with you. He's not relating to us based upon our performance.

Heavenly Father, I believe my faith in Jesus has made me clean and set apart to serve you without fear and condemnation!
Amen!

DAY 100

God Hears and Delivers Us

Oh, magnify the Lord with me, and let us exalt His name together. I sought the Lord, and He heard me, and delivered me from all my fears.

(Psalm 34:3–4)

Over the last one hundred days, I have shared with you what I consider to be significant truths available to us as we serve our living God. I trust it has blessed you to read these, and I hope you have been able to meditate on the truth I have shared in order to assimilate it for your own illumination.

The word "magnify" means "to enlarge" or make bigger.[14] The way we magnify the Lord is by thanking Him and praising Him for what He has done. We are not able to increase God's size or ability, but we are able to increase what He is able to do in us, in our experiences with Him. It all depends upon the way we see Him. I own a set of binoculars that will magnify up to thirty power. When I view an object through the optic, the object appears to come close and enlarges in my view. If I turn the

14 "Magnify," *Merriam-Webster Online Dictionary* (Merriam-Webster, Incorporated, 2021), https://www.merriam-webster.com/dictionary/magnify.

binocular around and view through the wrong end, everything becomes small and distant.

Whatever you focus on becomes bigger, and what you neglect becomes small. **God is who He is regardless of what you think, but He can only be to you what you believe Him to be.** If you believe God is small and weak, it doesn't mean God is small or weak. It just means you will have a small, weak God because He can only be to you what you believe Him to be.

As you focus upon Him, God becomes big, and your problems become small. You will see Him as bigger than any mountain (problem) you can or cannot see! Problems will shrink in comparison to our big and gracious God! As you stay focused upon our Father and your relationship with Him, you will find your confidence soars. As you seek Him, He will hear you and will deliver you from all your fears!

As you complete this devotional today, I invite you to *"...magnify the Lord with me, and let us exalt His name together..."* Would you take a few moments right now to reflect on the good things God has done? Remember some of the benefits I have described in this devotional, then thank and praise God for them. Always thank God things are as good as they are; it could always be worse!

Father be magnified through me as I praise and thank you for all You have done!

Amen!

Appendix:

PRAYERS

Prayer for Salvation

If you cannot remember a time when you prayed to confess Jesus as Lord and Savior, you are gambling with your life. If you are not born again and would like to be, you can pray the following prayer. I am lending you the words, but you need to sincerely mean them in your heart.

Heavenly Father, I believe You sent Jesus to die for my sins. I believe You raised Him from the dead and I choose Jesus today. I confess that Jesus is my Lord. I ask You to forgive me of my sins. I now turn away from my past, and I turn to You to live for You for the rest of my life. Thank you for loving me, for forgiving me, and for saving me.
In Jesus' name, I pray...
Amen!

Congratulations! This begins your new relationship with God as a new creature in Christ Jesus!

Prayer to Receive the Baptism with the Holy Spirit

The Promise of the Father is available to every believer. If you have made Jesus your personal Lord and Savior, the next step for you is to go ahead and receive the baptism with the Holy Spirit. The greatest thing I have ever received from the Lord, next to the forgiveness of my sins and salvation, is when I was filled with the Holy Spirit.

I encourage you to pray the following prayer in faith, believing to receive the baptism with the Holy Spirit. Expect God to fill you and expect Him to give you an utterance of other tongues in your spirit. Then cooperate with Him by faith using your mouth, voice, and tongue to articulate the utterance by faith. Remember, the Holy Spirit does not speak in tongues. He gives the utterance, and you will speak it forth.

Will you do it? If you will, then you will. If you won't, you won't. You have to be willing to cooperate and receive it by faith. God will do His part. He's not the variable. Pray the following prayer in faith believing:

Heavenly Father, I come to You to receive the gift of the Promise of the Father. I'm asking You to baptize me with

Your Spirit right now with the evidence of speaking with
other tongues. I thank you that You hear me, and You have
filled me with Your Spirit. I receive it now.
In Jesus' name, I pray...
Amen!

Some syllables from a language you have never learned will rise up from your spirit. As you speak them out loud by faith, you are releasing God's power from within. If you believed in your heart that you received from Him, God's Word promises you did. Now exercise it regularly. This isn't simply a one-time experience! May God bless you richly!

If you have received the baptism with the Holy Spirit today, we would love to hear about it. Please contact us using the information located at the end of this book.

Index of Scriptures

Day 51	Luke 1:35	**Day 76**	1 Pet. 4:10
Day 52	Eph. 3:14–16	**Day 77**	Jer. 29:11
Day 53	Heb 10:14–16	**Day 78**	2 Pet 1:2–4
Day 54	John 14:16–17	**Day 79**	Matt. 5:4
Day 55	John 16:7–9	**Day 80**	Psa. 27:13–14
Day 56	John 6:63	**Day 81**	Psa. 89:33–34
Day 57	John 7:37–39	**Day 82**	1 Thes. 4:14
Day 58	1 Cor 6:19–20	**Day 83**	Acts 7:55–56
Day 59	Gal. 5:22–23	**Day 84**	Rom. 5:1
Day 60	Eph. 1:13	**Day 85**	Eph. 1:6
Day 61	Eph. 4:30	**Day 86**	Matt. 6:25
Day 62	Acts 5:3–4	**Day 87**	Psa. 119:105
Day 63	Rom 8:26–27	**Day 88**	Pro. 4:20–22
Day 64	1 Cor 2:9–10	**Day 89**	Matt. 6:33
Day 65	Acts 9:31	**Day 90**	Isa. 33:6
Day 66	Psa. 103:1––2	**Day 91**	John 14:9
Day 67	Psa. 103:1-3	**Day 92**	Pro. 18:10
Day 68	Psa. 103:2-3	**Day 93**	1 Pet. 5:7
Day 69	Psa. 103:4	**Day 94**	Psa. 91:1–2
Day 70	Psa. 103:5	**Day 95**	Phil. 1:6
Day 71	Tit. 3:4–5	**Day 96**	Jos. 1:9
Day 72	John 12:26	**Day 97**	1 Cor. 2:16
Day 73	Gal. 4:6	**Day 98**	2 Cor. 9:8
Day 74	Isa. 54:9–10	**Day 99**	1 Cor. 1:2
Day 75	Psa. 107:1	**Day 100**	Psa. 34:3–4

References

"Accept." 2021. Merriam-Webster Online Dictionary. Merriam-Webster, Incorporated. 2021. https://www.merriam-webster.com/dictionary/accept.

"Dismay." 2021. In *Merriam-Webster Online Dictionary*. Merriam-Webster, Incorporated. https://www.merriam-webster.com/dictionary/dismay.

"Greek: Agonizomai." 2021. *Online Bible Commentary* - Andrew Wommack Ministries. 2021. https://www.awmi.net/reading/online-bible-commentary/?bn=1-timothy&cn=6&vn=12.

"H7965 - *Šālôm* - *Strong's Hebrew Lexicon* (KJV)." 2021. -Strong's Hebrew Lexicon (KJV). 2021. https://www.blueletterbible.org/lang/lexicon/lexicon.cfm?t=kjv&strongs=h7965.

"Magnify." 2021. *Merriam-Webster Online Dictionary*. Merriam-Webster, Incorporated. 2021. https://www.merriam-webster.com/dictionary/magnify.

"Manifold." 2021. *Merriam-Webster Online Dictionary*. Merriam-Webster, Incorporated. 2021. https://www.merriam-webster.com/dictionary/manifold.

"Strong's Greek: 243." 2021. Bible Hub. 2021. https://biblehub.com/greek/243.htm.

"Strong's Greek: 3076." 2021. Biblehub. 2021. https://biblehub. com/greek/3076.htm.

"Strong's Greek: 3140. Μαρτυρέω (Martureó)." 2021. Bible Hub. 2021. https://biblehub.com/greek/3140.htm.

"Strong's Greek: G37 - Sanctified." 2021. *King James Bible Dictionary*. 2021. http://kingjamesbibledictionary.com/ StrongsNo/G37/sanctified.

"Strong's Greek: 4318." 2021. Bible Hub. 2021. https://biblehub. com/greek/4318.htm.

"Strong's Hebrew: 4832." 2021. Bible Hub. 2021. https://bible-hub.com/hebrew/4832.htm.

"Strongs's #4878:" 2021. Bible Tools. 2021. https://www.bible-tools.org/index.cfm/fuseaction/Lexicon.show/ID/G4878/ sunantilambanomai.htm.

"Strongs's #4972." 2021. Bible Tools. 2021. https://www.bible-tools.org/index.cfm/fuseaction/Lexicon.show/ID/G4972/ sphragizo.htm.

The Holy Bible: Amplified Bible [AMP]. 2015. La Habra, Califor-nia: The Lockman Foundation. https://www.biblegateway. com/versions/Amplified-Bible-AMP/#booklist.

The Holy Bible: King James Version [KJV]. 1999. New York, NY: American Bible Society. Public Domain.

The Holy Bible: New International Version [NIV]. 1984. Grand Rapids: Zonderman Publishing House. https://www.biblegateway.com/versions/ New-International-Version-NIV-Bible/#booklist.

The Holy Bible: The New King James Version [NKJV]. 1999. Nashville, TN: Thomas Nelson, Inc. https://www.biblegateway.com/versions/ New-King-James-Version-NKJV-Bible/#booklist.

About the Author

Mike was born again at twenty years of age. At the age of thirty, he answered the call of God to the ministry and began pastoring. He is a graduate of Christ for the Nations Institute in Dallas, TX, as well as Charis Bible College in Woodland Park, CO. He earned his Doctor of Ministry in Theology from Life Christian University in Lutz, FL.

Over the course of the years, Mike has pastored two churches and has served as the Chaplain at the Kyle Correctional Center in Kyle, TX, since 1999. In addition, he has held the position of Director of Life Christian Bible Institute Austin/Lockhart since 2006.

Mike's call is to teach the Word of God in a way that every believer is able to understand and apply to their lives. He is especially anointed to teach and lead believers to receive the baptism with the Holy Spirit with the evidence of speaking in other tongues. His straightforward explanation makes it easy for believers to receive the "Promise of the Father". He also has a passion for teaching the Kingdom of God with an emphasis on grace and faith.

Mike lives with his wife Stephanie in Central Texas. In addition to his love for the Word of God, Mike has many hobbies that he enjoys. He competes in Cowboy Action Shooting, rides his motorcycle in the Texas hill country with his wife, and enjoys serving up authentic Texas BBQ. He also enjoys woodworking when he has the time.

Mike McComb Ministries
P.O. Box 365
Lockhart, TX 78644
mikemccombministries@gmail.com
www.mikemccombministries.com

CPSIA information can be obtained
at www.ICGtesting.com
Printed in the USA
LVHW081416160222
711304LV00023B/273